Coaching Women's Softball

Coaching Women's Softball
A Practical Guide with Insights from Players

STEVE MEYER

Foreword by Taylor Harkins

McFarland & Company, Inc., Publishers
Jefferson, North Carolina

All photographs courtesy of the sports information offices at each coach's college or university, unless otherwise noted.

ISBN (print) 978-1-4766-8558-8
ISBN (ebook) 978-1-4766-4308-3

LIBRARY OF CONGRESS AND BRITISH LIBRARY
CATALOGUING DATA ARE AVAILABLE

Library of Congress Control Number 2021022109

© 2021 Steve Meyer. All rights reserved

No part of this book may be reproduced or transmitted in any form or by any means, electronic or mechanical, including photocopying or recording, or by any information storage and retrieval system, without permission in writing from the publisher.

Front cover: Former Samford University all-conference pitcher Susanna Meyer in her windup (courtesy Susanna Meyer)

Printed in the United States of America

McFarland & Company, Inc., Publishers
Box 611, Jefferson, North Carolina 28640
www.mcfarlandpub.com

Table of Contents

Foreword by Taylor Harkins   1

Introduction   3

1. Connecting Is Essential   9
2. Must They Love Their Teammates?   28
3. Loving Your Players   45
4. Leading Your Players   70
5. Praise and Appreciation   87
6. Controlling Selfish Players   106
7. Respect Is Everything   120
8. Know the Game   134
9. A Coach's Agenda   147
10. Profiles in Great Coaching   156

Index   175

Foreword
by Taylor Harkins

I was a softball player. I was a college softball player. I loved the game and everything about it. I loved the competition. I loved working towards a goal. I loved the games, and oddly even loved the practices. It seems simple—just a kid that loves a game. However, no kid becomes great at a game without someone to lead and teach her—and that person brings a whole new dynamic to that relationship with the game.

A former coach once shared a quote with me stating, "Boys have to play good to feel good, and girls have to feel good to play good"—and as I got older, I realized how true this was. Even more so, I realized how much a coach can affect how a female player feels, and therefore how she performs.

I saw how the great coaches could take my successes to new heights. I felt empowered when my leaders believed in me, and I knew they had my back, regardless of a bad day on the field. They saw me as a person, not just a player. The greatest coaches earned my respect by their honesty and integrity. They were relatable by their transparency and vulnerability. They coached in a constructive manner. Once I knew they cared for and respected me, it was mutual, and I'd run through a brick wall for them. I thrived on the open communication and felt encouraged to talk about my losses and defeats knowing I would feel better after a discussion with them. I was confident they had my best interest at heart, and I knew nothing I did on the field would change how they felt about me as a person. I could play the game I loved with all of the confidence in the world, and when I was confident, the opportunities for success were endless.

Contrarily, I saw the effects of selfish and negative coaches, and how quickly their words and actions could inhibit my performance. In these situations, I felt their respect for me was conditional on how I performed, and that completely stole my confidence. I was soon playing in

Foreword by Taylor Harkins

fear, paralyzed with anxiety, and my performance had a ceiling that kept lowering over time. I felt my bad performances only distanced myself from those coaches, and a bad day on the field changed the way they felt about me personally. I didn't feel comfortable communicating with them, and my love for the game began to slip away.

I share these experiences to belabor how important a coach's platform is. A coach is a leader by default, but also someone that shares the love of the same game with the players, someone that can celebrate the wins while truly understanding the path it took to get there, and someone who feels the same raw pain and hurt of the losses and setbacks. They have all the tools to reach players on a deep level, if they just use them the right way. As a player, when you rely on someone to lead you, the character and actions of the leader become far more monumental in a player's career than you can imagine. It can make or break their love for the game, and more importantly can build up or tear them down emotionally. As athletes and coaches, we can all agree that sports are much more than a game. Sports teach us lessons that we carry with us, even after our playing careers are over. Similarly, coaches are shaping their players far beyond their athletic identities, whether they might realize it or not.

I had the privilege of playing for Steve Meyer a large portion of my career, and he was every word of the great coaches I described previously. I met him at a pivotal point in my career—a pivotal point in my life, for that matter—so to say he has played a big part in my life is an understatement. Even at a young age, because of him, I started to understand how a great coach could change my outlook of the game. He lifted me up, but also pushed me to get better, and most importantly, I never had to wonder if he cared about me, respected me, or believed in me. He never let me settle and was a huge reason I played college softball. As a result, the little girl he believed in, that doubted herself more often than not, went on to have a career she can look back on and be proud of.

I was lucky to have more great coaches along the way than the contrary; therefore I can say with confidence from personal experience—it undeniably changed my life and shaped who I am today.

Former Birmingham Southern College (BSC) Panther Taylor Harkins was the conference Pitcher of the Year and a four time All Conference selection. The former BSC Female Athlete of the Year graduated in 2017 with a degree in accounting and works for a large accounting firm in Birmingham, Alabama.

Introduction

For many decades, coaches from t-ball dads to Division I college coaches have been coaching girls the only way they knew how: like boys. At some point, despite the differences between the sexes, coaches decided that when it came to coaching, the players must be alike. Female coaches, raised under this one-size-fits-all system, also coached in the manner they had learned, coaching women as if they were men.

Dr. Jason Tee, Ph.D., is a sports scientist affiliated with Carnegie Coach Education, a coaching education and certification organization located in Leeds, U.K., that instructs over 3,000 coaches every year from a variety of sports. His words ring true across all sports including woman's softball: "I'm pretty clear on one thing. The wrong approach is to treat the females like males. One of the key coaching tenets promoted by our own Carnegie Sports Coaching academic group is the what and the how is fundamentally influenced by the who. The challenge is that the differences between men and women are often subtle, and so the implications of these differences are not always obvious."*

Before I began my college coaching career, I worked in law enforcement as a police officer in Miami, and then for 23 years as a special agent with the Federal Bureau of Explosives, Alcohol, Tobacco and Firearms (ATF). During those years, I interviewed or interrogated hundreds of criminals. I don't know everything, but I do know that if I went into an interview room without an understanding of the guy across the table from me, my chances of getting anywhere with him were almost zero. However, if I went in armed with knowledge of what he really wanted and what would get his attention, my chances of getting the cooperation I sought would skyrocket.

One thing is for certain: if we as coaches want to have the best

---

*Jason Tee, "Coaching Female Athletes: What's Really Different?" *carnegieXchange: School of Sport* (blog), January 6, 2018, https://www.leedsbeckett.ac.uk/blogs/carnegie-xchange/2018/06/coaching-female-athletes—whats-really-different/.

Introduction

chance of success, we had better have a pretty good understanding of the players we are coaching. Otherwise we stay in our comfort zone, taking our same knowledge and behaviors into season after season, wondering why our players don't fully respond to us. Although we may take some measures to upgrade our knowledge of the game, we often ignore the elephant in the room: that we really don't know much about reaching and bringing out the best in the players in our charge.

Coach Anson Dorrance, Head Coach, University of North Carolina Women's Soccer, 1986 USA Olympic Women's Soccer Coach, and author of *The Vision of a Champion*, writes of the challenges inherent in coaching female athletes:

> Coaching women therefore can be said to combine some attributes of what you know of athletics to be universally true (i.e., competition), with the more subtle, or artful, aspects of leadership. If you are capable of leading women effectively, I genuinely believe you will have evolved to a much higher level of humanity. This is because you are forced to develop a connected leadership style that is much richer and more satisfying than the hierarchal style that pervades so much of male leadership. In fact, this more connective style is the direction into which our entire culture is evolving.*

Dr. Cheri Toledo, a former high school and college coach, explains the subtle yet powerful differences of communicating effectively with the female athlete: "Since there are differences in the way men and women think, effectively coaching girls and women to their optimal levels of performance dictates that male coaches study those differences."†

Knowing the differences between the male and female athlete can be the key to rebooting our coaching philosophy and practices. With new understandings, we can abandon methods that are tailored to males and begin to embrace those that are female specific.

In this book we examine the female softball player, what motivates her, what she really wants from her coach and from her sport. We explore the differences between her and her male counterpart, and what that means for those who coach them. You will hear from many of them, including a four-time Olympian, as well as All-American and

---

*Anson Dorrance, "Coaching Women: Going Against the Instincts of My Gender," Amherst Soccer Association, http://www.amherstsoccer.com/coaching-corner/coaching-women-going-against-the-instincts-of-my-gender.

†Kim Constantinesco, "Timeout Q&A: Men Coaching Girls and Women," *Purpose 2 Play*, March 14, 2015, https://purpose2play.com/coaches-corner/timeout-qa-men-coaching-girls-and-women/.

Introduction

All-Conference players who shared their experiences with coaches, some that were memorable and some that were not.

Successful college coaches weigh in, giving us insights and experiences that teach us about connecting, motivating, and winning with female athletes. We will explore what it means to love our players and to lead them in a way that resonates with them.

What you learn may not fit into your coaching model. It may challenge you to take another look at your assumptions about how to teach, motivate, and lead female athletes.

The question you may have as a reader and as a coach is why should you consider my thoughts on coaching females, since I obviously approach the subject as a male? The question is a valid one, and I am happy to address it.

First of all, the book comes from a place of concern over the fact that female softball players are not always being treated as they should, as athletes and, in some cases, as people. My feelings for players (present and future), compelled me to research and write this book. I wanted to allow female softball players to speak through the book, hence the inclusion of 50 female player interviews, a survey of 139 players from all divisions, and the inclusion of input from 9 female college coaches of the 22 who contributed.

The knowledge I have gathered through many years of coaching female athletes, starting with my daughters and ending with college athletes, is poured into every chapter without an agenda. I believe that the conclusions are true and stand alone, devoid of any male bias or condescension. The important thing to me is that the information in this book could revolutionize the way we coach female softball athletes.

I wish to thank the many college softball players who participated in the anonymous survey referenced in the book. Additionally, the following players shared their specific experiences and thoughts related to coaching and coaches, and are quoted in the book:

Emily Merritt—Birmingham Southern College
Taylor Harkins—Birmingham Southern College
Alex Scene—Birmingham Southern College
Savanna Lee—Birmingham Southern College
Torri Garner—Birmingham Southern College
Ronnie Ferris—Birmingham Southern College
Chelsea Fernandez—Birmingham Southern College

Introduction

Brittany Berkopec—Birmingham Southern College
Bethany Fronk Mingo—Birmingham Southern College
Taylor Bassett—Birmingham Southern College
Amanda Bellow—Birmingham Southern College
Beth Lefter—Birmingham Southern College
Ashley Bice Culliver—Birmingham Southern College
Taylor Anderson—Birmingham Southern College
Whitney Gillespie—Jacksonville State University
Sarah Borders—Jacksonville State University
Taylor Moon—Belmont University
Cristin Vitak Wafer—Baylor University
Amanda Lochte—Texas Lutheran University
Kassie Maddox—Texas Lutheran University
Nicole Snow—Texas Lutheran University
Kyla Lockley—Texas Lutheran University
Cassie Roche—Texas Lutheran University
Lauren Myers—Texas Lutheran University
Kaymee Gooden—Texas Lutheran University
Maitlin Raycroft—Texas Lutheran University
Jennifer Gallagher—Texas Lutheran University
Paige Riddick—Wallace State Community College/
  Shorter University
Sallie Van Kirk—Wallace State Community College/UAB
Morgan Farmer Byers—William Peace University
Summer Greer Smith—William Peace University
Summer Jacobs—William Peace University
Niki Dobbins—William Peace University
Kaitlyn Hasty—Christopher Newport University
Savannah Couch—Christopher Newport University
Brooke Wyderski—University of Wisconsin
Heather Rudnicki—University of Wisconsin
Stephanie Lombardo—University of Wisconsin
Kayla Konwent—University of Wisconsin
Angela Morrow—University of Wisconsin
Sydney McCormick—Trevecca Nazarene University
MacKray Odom—Trevecca Nazarene University
Jenna Lilley—University of Oregon
Gven Svekis—University of Oregon
Lauren Lindvall—University of Oregon
Janelle Lindvall—University of Oregon

Introduction

Hannah Vines—Huntingdon College
Morgan Arst—East Texas Baptist University
Kelly McLendon—East Texas Baptist University
Susanna Meyer—Samford University

My heartfelt appreciation goes out to the generous coaches who graciously volunteered to contribute their thoughts to this book. These great coaches, representing all NCAA divisions as well as JUCO have much in common. In addition to having a passion for our sport, they understand the importance of connecting with, loving, and leading our young athletes. They are committed to valuing their players on and off the field, during college and beyond. Their players are blessed beyond measure to have them as coaches.

Jana McGinnis—Jacksonville State University
Joe Guthrie—University of Alabama at Birmingham
Courtnay Foster—University of Alabama at Birmingham
Jimmy Kolaitis—Arizona State University
Tracy Grindrod—Snead State Community College
Ben Tyree—Trevecca Nazarene University
Wade Wilson—Texas Lutheran University
Keith Parr—Christopher Newport University
Kimball Cassady—Birmingham Southern College
Michael Reed—University of Texas Tyler
Charlie Dobbins—William Peace University
Janae Shirley—East Texas Baptist University
Brandon Elliot—Virginia Wesleyan University
Beverly Smith—University of South Carolina
Glenn Moore—Baylor University
Laura Berg—University of Oregon
Danielle Zymkowitz—University of Wisconsin
Craig Snyder—Texas A&M University
Megan Rhodes Smith—University of Tennessee
J.J. Dillingham—Lipscomb University
Casey Chrietzberg—Huntingdon College
Mike Davenport—University of North Georgia

Chapter 1

Connecting Is Essential

"With women, your effectiveness is through your ability to relate," Anson Dorrance, Head Coach of the University of North Carolina Women's Soccer and 1986 USA Olympic Women's Soccer Coach, says. "They have to feel that you care about them personally or have some kind of connection with them beyond the game ... to be an effective leader of a men's team, you don't need personal rapport as long as there is respect. That's the extent of the relationship. That's all that's really required. But in a women's team, respect is only part of it, and it is derived from a relationship. Women have to have a sense that you care for them above and beyond their (athletic) abilities."*

Coach Dorrance is telling us something that our players already know. While respect for their coach may suffice for the male athlete, female athletes require a connection. Without that connection they seek with their coach, they will be dissatisfied. That lack of a connection can impact their motivation and limit their performance. An All-American, record-holding home-run hitter explains just how foundational the coach-player connection is to success: "I think coaches overlook that they have to make the player feel special and significant before they even step on to the field. If they don't do this beforehand then they won't ever reach the player or motivate her to perform at 100%."

Connecting with an audience is something done by everyone, from a politician to a preacher to an appliance salesman. Stand-up comedians are masters at it. Yet somehow, we as coaches often don't consider it critical to connect with our "audience." My son spent his younger years as a stand-up comedian. I often accompanied him as he appeared in clubs around the country or taped specials in front of a live audience. The most critical time of his comedy set was the first 20 seconds. The audience was testing him—could he connect

---

*Michelle Amidon, "Coaching Strategies for Communicating and Motivating Female Athletes," April 28, 2016, https://www.usahockey.com/news_article/show/642676-coaching-strategies-for-communicating-and-motivating-female-athletes.

with them or not? Our players are asking the same question: can we connect?

The need to connect to their coach is something virtually all players identified as essential to optimum performance. Ninety-eight percent of college softball players surveyed marked "True" to the statement: "I perform best when I play for a coach who connects with me." If connecting with our players occupied a slot lower on our priority list, we need to move it up. Way up.

It is interesting that in the follow up statement: "My coach made a strong effort to connect with me," only 72 percent indicated that this was true. Now, 72 percent doesn't sound too bad until you realize that almost 30 percent of players are operating at less than their best because their coach failed to connect with them. While 98 percent of players want and need connection from us as coaches, only 7 out of 10 feel that they are getting it. Thankfully, connecting with our players is a matter we can do something about.

An individual connection between you as the coach and every player on the team is essential to success. An inside joke, knowledge of their family situation, interest in their goals outside of sports, appreciation of talents or skills unrelated to athletics, these are only some of the areas we must drill into to make a connection. We must look for anything that shows that we are interested enough to find that key to a personal connection. This is what it takes to make our players feel valued.

When we talk about connecting, we are referring to a long-term endeavor, something that takes ongoing effort and maintenance. An All-Conference pitcher explains: "Coaches I have connected with have all shared similar qualities and characteristics. The most important would be *consistently* taking interest in my personal life outside of the sport. All coaches can start off asking about your personal life much like saying 'hey how are you' when you run into someone you know in the grocery store. It is more of a formality. But making an effort to keep up with someone as you would a close friend shows the person you truly care, and in turn creates trust."

Arizona State Assistant Coach and nationally recognized hitting guru Jimmy Kolaitis speaks of specific ways he and his staff connect with their athletes:

> Today's athletes need to know you care, and sometimes just telling them is not enough. We must show them that we care. So how do we do this?

Chapter 1. Connecting Is Essential

1. Have a conversation, learn about what interests them outside of softball. Learn about their family and where they come from.
2. Write a personalized note—on how much you appreciate them as people.
3. Invite them over for dinner, so they get to see that coaches are humans too.
4. Have conversation about their future. Help them reach their goals outside of softball.

We can't afford to leave forming meaningful connections to chance. By having a strategy in place, we pursue our athletes, determined to form the bond that we both need in order to be successful.

Connecting is something we can't fake, at least not for long. It takes work to find that common ground, to get on the same wavelength. It takes effort to observe enough about our players' distinctives to be able to know how to connect. Picking up on the cues they provide, we must know their differences and connect with them where they are. For example, if a player is extremely private and is uncomfortable when her personal space is violated, we need to know that. If she is ultra sensitive to teasing, we need to adjust how we connect with her.

Now, we can hold fast to the notion that we have "our way" of connecting, and that the players need to connect with us, not the other way around. In having this attitude, we ensure that our team will not reach its potential. Furthermore, even if we are great technical coaches and

Jimmy Kolaitis (left) with an unidentified umpire, 2019.

have recruited a team of standout players, there are teams out there with all that, plus a coach who connects with his or her players. Against that team, I don't like our chances of winning.

An All-Region outfielder recognized the importance of coaches working hard to find that connection with each player:

> Each coach should strive for at least a single connection point between themselves and each player. Find out what makes them "tick." Find out how they were coached in younger years. Find out how involved their parents were in their athletic development and did the player respond positively or negatively to this coaching. Is the player looking to avoid confrontation and not giving full effort out of fear of being criticized or are they not giving full effort because it has never been required of them or may they don't know what their maximum potential is. Each coach should look to connect to these individuals on whatever level they are starting at and adjust fluidly to bring the team together so that the unit responds to the coach.

This outstanding athlete understood what many coaches do not: that we must figure out how to connect with players no matter their personality or athletic prowess. We are to "look to connect to these individuals on whatever level they are starting on." Some players are extroverts, and connecting with us as coaches is easy for them and for us. These are engaging people who are used to connecting with their coaches as well as just about everyone. We can become satisfied when we are connected with a good portion of our team, rationalizing that the rest of them have some sort of problem. We've got to work harder to bring ourselves and our message to the players who keep us at arm's length and are resistant to connecting, perhaps because they have never been approached.

Snead State Community College Head Coach Tracy Grindrod makes the point that connection forms the foundation for leadership. Coach Grindrod previously coached Wallace State Community College to the National Championships in 2008 and 2013. He is a highly sought-out clinician and teacher of our sport. As a retired United States Army First Sergeant, he speaks from a wealth of leadership experience: "Leading today's athlete has many challenges. Being able to reach them and keep them working to improve each day and contribute to the team's success requires a dedicated effort on each coach and player's part. Connection is a first step. Finding what each is interested in and being able to have conversations about the things they are interested in

Chapter 1. Connecting Is Essential

opens the door for motivation, commitment and dedication for today's female athlete."

I know a college pitching coach who was in the process of figuring out how to connect with his freshman pitchers. As he chatted with one of them before a fall practice, he asked her what kind of music she liked and what her favorite song was. Oddly enough her answer was the 1960's rock song "Hey Joe" by Jimi Hendrix. This smart coach added the song to the practice music mix that played during her afternoon bullpen session. When the unmistakable guitar rift of the introduction to "Hey Joe" blared across the loudspeakers, the pitcher met eyes with the coach. Mission accomplished, connection made.

Some players obviously present a bigger challenge when it comes to forming a connection. For the distant, the hypersensitive to criticism, or the angry individual on your team, look to the dynamic she has with her parents. She may have been subject to an undue amount of criticism growing up and was unable to gain much approval. Without going beyond casual observation, much understanding can be gained about this person you must reach for the next four years.

As any educator will tell you, the connection between the teacher and the learner determines the extent of the transfer of knowledge. In other words, we may be the world's foremost experts in our sport, but if

Tracy Grindrod, 2019.

Coaching Women's Softball

we lack a connection with our female athletes, very little learning takes place. Our connection earns us our opening to teach. Without teaching, there is no improvement. Our lifetime of valuable knowledge can be effectively wasted. We are speaking, explaining, and correcting all right, but without a connection we are talking to the wind.

Texas A&M Assistant Coach Craig Snyder addresses connecting with the current generation of players, designated by the letter "Z." The 19-year coaching veteran and member of the coaching staff of the 2018 NCAA National Champions Florida State Seminoles encourages us to connect with them outside of the softball field:

> Generation Z has presented different challenges for parents and coaches. "They're different, they don't get it, their lazy, or they just aren't being raised right." I have heard all these statements about generation Z. What we often forget is our parents said the same thing about us growing up! And guess what? Their parents said the same about them and so forth! You see each generation is raising children differently. There is no map or "Parenting for Dummies" book that will guide us.
>
> What we do know about Generation Z is they're knowledgeable and cautious. They have world's answers at the tip of their fingers, or shall I say in their palm. Technology such as phones, ipads, tablets, etc. have given them the power to find answers. But they're also cautious. They now the see world for what it is. They see bombings, plane crashes, shootings. I our kids are now growing up in a world where it's not safe to go to school or even church because of the fear of it being attacked by a gunman. It's different. So they may need us for answers as much, but they sure need us for hope. Napoleon Bonaparte once said, "A Leader is a dealer in hope."
>
> So how do we connect? There are so many different ways to go about this, but target a few ways I have seen connection grow. Given the information and facts presented above, we must do things outside of ball. I have seen success in teams participating in things outside of the sport (softball in my case). We would take athletes out to do community service, such as cleaning up streets, visiting the sick or even volunteering at community events. You see, you get the real personality away from what is comfortable. It's easy to have your guard up at practice. That's comfortable. But when you have to speak to a group of cancer patients about persevering, then you have to learn the value of being comfortable being uncomfortable. As a leader and coach, you start developing these connections by helping through these moments. They start to see how much you care for the person and not just the ball player. When you start getting to these moments you see connection start forming.
>
> There are numerous ways to connect with your players. Music,

Chapter 1. Connecting Is Essential

family, food or any common interests. Again, they want to know you care about them as players. Don't be the old coach who never tries to understand Generation Z. If you start a sentence with "Well, back in my day...," then you will quickly lose these athletes. Coaching is caring and they want to know you care.

Highly regarded clinician and teacher Joe Guthrie, currently Head Coach at the University of Alabama at Birmingham (UAB) shares his experience about what a difference connecting makes in terms of outcome:

In the summer of 2013, I was hired as an assistant softball coach at Penn State University. The entire athletic program had recently been rocked by the fallout from the Jerry Sandusky scandal. My prior experience coaching women's softball had only been starting a program from scratch at Marion Military Institute for the previous six years. I had never seen a fractured community like PSU was at that time. This distrust penetrated the ranks of our softball team too. In the end, gaining our athletes' trust would prove to be one of the most valuable lessons I learned from this experience.

As the 2013–14 year progressed, our staff and I made great progress sharing our knowledge of the game with the players. Some individual numbers on defense and offense were better. Ultimately, we did not improve the number of wins at Penn State that first year. Why? One reason: we concluded through athlete interviews and surveys that we had

Craig Snyder, 2020.

spent far more time improving our on field instruction and little time getting to know our players.

From the very beginning of the 2014–15 season, we made getting to know players a priority. We started with each coach sitting in small groups with players and simply spending time getting to know one another. Though some softball talk existed in the conversation, we mostly humanized one another through learning about relatives' names, personal goals, other items important to one another. Immediately, I began to find myself enjoying being around our players in any setting. I felt they began to show signs of working more cohesively and were more receptive to instruction. We would go on to be the eighth most improved team in the country that season winning 29 games. It would be the first winning season at Penn State since before the scandal and change forever how I viewed my priorities as a coach.

The implication of Coach Guthrie's experience at Penn State was that relationships with the players played a much larger role in winning than did technical instruction. To be sure, some coaches have more knowledge than others, and having such knowledge may make them feel special about themselves, but it's not enough. Unless you connect, the great things you are teaching in practice have a limited effect.

An All-Conference pitcher at a well-known Division I program talks about a very special coach and his commitment to her through tough times. This connection went beyond softball and beyond winning. This coach took upon himself the role of a trusted friend, concerned for this player's mental, physical, emotional, and spiritual well-being:

> I was at the age where you consider marriage or where you begin to choose future candidates as a spouse. I ended up choosing the wrong one to be with and found myself in a situation that was full of violence, hurt, and suffering. Many people made comments such as, "Why don't you just leave?" The only thing I could ever respond with was, "It's not that simple." I was stuck in a relationship of fear, verbal/physical abuse, and just pure evil. I came to the decision of hiding the abuse as a student-athlete. I felt like I should keep it from my team, coaches and community due to the fact of being fearful, embarrassed, and defeated.
>
> From the outside looking in, it seemed like nobody even noticed the change that was apparent in my demeanor, priorities, and physically. Only one person noticed these changes about one year into the relationship. Little did I know that this coach would help change my life forever. He started asking me, "Are you all right lately?" I knew by him asking, he was aware that I was in a rough spot. I noticed that my coach became

Chapter 1. Connecting Is Essential

Joe Guthrie, 2019.

observant with me; he would talk to me more often and check in on my "mental health." He was concerned for my well-being as a person, not just a player.

This coach became a major influence in my life, but it took time for me to build up my trust in men. I realized over time that he cared more about the person I was becoming, rather than the softball player that I was. My entire life I was always talked about as "the athlete" or "the pitcher," and when the abuse became visible, I became "weak" in other's eyes. Teammates and friends walked away, my parents had no idea on what else to do, and I felt alone and defeated.

My coach and ONE teammate stayed. Two people kept trying to save me. That was it.

After two years of fighting and trying to escape, these two people saved me. They introduced me to the one who could take it all away; our Lord and Savior. It took two years of defeat for me to find the everlasting love of God. After living a life full of secrets and abuse, I was fortunate enough to have a coach that went the extra mile to make sure that I was safe, secure, and protected. He taught me that my worth was so much more than what I was receiving from worldly things, such as a boyfriend or success in softball. He opened up my eyes to see that God created me in His eyes and I needed to treat myself right. My eyes were opened up to see that God had better things planned for my life. Without this coach, there is no telling where I would be right now; I don't even want to imagine the outcome. My coach showed me God's everlasting love that changed my life forever.

Thank you, Coach.

Coaching Women's Softball

This coach did what we all dream of doing, or at least we should. He changed the trajectory of a young life and helped someone make hard choices.

In recruiting, connecting with athletes and their families is an absolute must. First impressions reign supreme, and much rides on our initial meeting. If you are able to connect with a highly sought recruit better than the coach of another school also vying for this player, you have a great chance of landing her. If we just go through the motions, with little effort spent on connecting, banking on the nice facilities and new freshman dorms to seal the deal, we have probably lost her. Whether or not we are able to connect might be the most important factor in a recruit's decision to commit to play for us. If there is no connection, the young person may not be able to envision playing for us.

An All-American first baseman tells of how a college coach began connecting with her long before she began her college career:

> I connected with my assistant coach my freshman year in college, honestly before freshman year even began. He made an effort to show me I was important before I even started college. He would reach out to me often to check in on me, even if it wasn't about softball. He would also find time in his own busy schedule, during spring season, to come and watch me play as well. After beginning college, he continued to make an effort to show me I was important. He always pointed out the good things I was doing in practice and in games. This has continued even after he was no longer my coach. He reaches out and checks in on me and is always there for me when I need advice. He first started as a coach and is now a dear friend.

If our efforts to connect with recruits are just a pretense, the athlete will realize this when she arrives on campus and begins college. The relationship building you begin during the recruiting process must be genuine and must continue once your recruit becomes your player.

There may be a situation during the recruiting process where none of the coaches on a staff are able to connect with a prospective player. This happened when we were recruiting a particular player who was also being actively recruited by another college. The coach of that program spoke to me of her experience with this player at a prospects camp they held. She told me that while they saw this athlete as a viable possibility, her sarcastic demeanor and resulting inability to connect with the coaching staff resulted in her being removed from their list of recruits. Knowing we were also recruiting this player, she tried to do me a favor

Chapter 1. Connecting Is Essential

by letting me know what I might be getting: a player that coaches cannot connect with. I foolishly ignored her counsel and proceeded to recruit and eventually commit to this player. Though she enjoyed some success on the field, she remained sarcastic and distant, never really opening up sufficiently to connect with.

We as coaches must at least attempt to connect with all of our players, including our nonstarters. If we have a connection with some players and not others, the ones left out will pick up on it. If they feel that we are favoring the ones they see and hear us connect with, jealousy will settle in to do its damage. This alone is enough for a player to undermine an entire team. If we connect with one, we must try to connect with all.

Another barrier to connecting we must overcome is the reliance on texting, Facebook, and other social media. This pseudo-communication just doesn't cut it when looking to establish real connections. Verbal, face-to-face communication is the foundation to form a connection. Maybe because we are in the world of 14- to 22-year-olds, we have become less dependent on real communication, instead texting hundreds of times a day and expressing our connection by liking their Facebook post. We can't afford to allow laziness to keep us from communicating and connecting the old-fashioned way: face to face listening, observing, and speaking.

In spite of our best efforts, there will be some players whom we will be unable to connect with. I once coached a very good player whose overbearing and controlling father rendered her a fragile, hypersensitive person. Just about any comment I made to her would be misconstrued as harsh criticism. She would take a neutral statement to heart, and it would render her useless on the field. We had to be very careful in how we delivered correction due to her extreme defensiveness. We went about going the extra mile to connect with her, working around her sensitivity to criticism. In the end, no amount of accommodation could overcome her aversion to receiving feedback. Following a strikeout, this player complained to her father, who was standing near the dugout, that I had made a mean comment to her for striking out on a change-up. To make a long story short, both player and father created quite a loud and dramatic scene resulting in the father being escorted off campus by security and the player being removed from the team.

For those of us who decide to do all we can to connect with our players, the rewards are great. Beyond success on the field, our connection will extend into the future, positively influencing our players for years to come. A standout Division I pitcher puts connecting into perspective:

> I remember every coach who took the time and effort to connect with me as a player. The ones who showed interest in who I was as a player and truly wanted to connect with me to help me realize my full potential made me want to perform better for them. I believe a part of my drive to get better every practice was greatly influenced by the coaches who connected with me. I wanted to do them proud. They stand out in my mind as great coaches simply because by purposely trying to connect with me not only helped me as a player but helped me as a person and coach as well.

An outfielder connected with her travel ball coach because this coach put forth effort. The player mentions specifics that are common to all real connections. She cared about her personally, and demonstrated her interest in her by pushing her to improve and by reaching out to college coaches for her.

> The ability to connect with a coach makes playing on a team that much better. For me, I was able to connect with my travel ball coach during my junior year of high school. She was someone I could relate to because she was fresh out of college and had experienced being a student athlete. She pushed me at practices to do stuff I never thought I would be able to do because she believed that I had what it took to play at the collegiate level. I was able to connect with her because she got to know me not only on the field but off the field and she wanted what was best for me. She took interest in where I wanted to go to school and she started contacting everyone on my list trying to make sure I got to attend a top school of my choice. Not all coaches would help you do this.

One thing is for sure: while we coach an entire team, our relationship, our connection is ultimately with individuals, and each point of connection is unique. Anson Dorrance, Head Coach University of North Carolina Women's Soccer, 1986 USA Olympic Women's Soccer Coach, and arguably the most successful male coach of female athletes in any sport, puts it this way: "Making connections is important. Men don't necessarily want a relationship to a coach. With women you need to establish a different relationship with each one. Some women don't want any kind of connection, while others require a closer and more caring relationship. Some want constant feedback; some don't want any. However, whatever the relationship is, it must be a relationship of their

Chapter 1. Connecting Is Essential

choosing. They will let you know what they need, or don't, and it is your job to respond."*

This uniqueness compels us to listen to each athlete, observe them in a variety of situations, and learn as much as possible about what makes them tick. Putting our daily to do lists aside, we look beyond what drills we are planning for practice to getting to know our players, one at a time. Meeting for a weekday lunch on campus or inviting her to stop by your office to chat are easy ways to begin to gather information on the player you are reaching out to. Going further, offer to watch her big presentation or attend a non-softball school event she is involved with.

A former two-time PAC 12 All-Region infielder writes of how an assistant coach connected with her:

> In college, I was fortunate enough to have connected with one of the assistant coaches. He was our hitting coach but helped tremendously with the mental aspect of the game as well. I connected with Coach for quite a few reasons but one huge reason, because we knew he cared. He had a big enough heart to care about us not only as players but as people, individuals. He didn't just care about how we performed on the field but he was consistently checking in with us and took time to know us as human beings, which is a key quality a coach can have, especially when coaching females.

The recurring theme of how these players best feel connected to a coach is expressed in her final sentence: "I find it to be very beneficial when a coach goes beyond a player and takes time to understand that player's general interests, personality and what it is that makes the athlete tick, and this is what this coach did."

A PAC 12 All-Region catcher and Team USA member traces her success back to a coach who cared enough to connect with her as both an athlete and as a person. His efforts to connect enabled her to receive his instruction and develop into someone who succeeded at the highest levels of softball:

> The first coach I truly connected with was the first adult in my life who I felt understood by. He took the time to get to know his players as people. He wanted to know about my home life, my interests other than softball, and always made me feel like he cared even when he probably didn't. In a short amount of time I felt comfortable, I could be myself, I WAS HAPPY. This was crucial for me at that age. There's no way I would have become the player I was without his encouragement

---
*Dorrance, "Coaching Women."

to be a secure, confident individual. Oh, and I forgot to mention ... he taught me almost everything I know about the game. None of that information regarding the game would have helped me or sank in like it did if that relationship hadn't been established in the first place.

Lipscomb University Assistant Coach J.J. Dillingham explains how he makes connecting with his players a top priority:

I think connecting with players is an important aspect of building trust with them regardless of the age you coach. I have been told numerous times that players don't care how much you know until they know how much you care. I find a lot of truth in that statement. It's very important for me to get to know our players on a personal level. I feel you really can't get a good grasp on how to coach a player until you get to know them. Each player is unique and what works for one may not work for another. I don't think you can have the same approach with each player. My job may be to coach them, but it's so much more than that. I want to make an impact on their lives during their time in our program. I believe their four years in college are the most influential of their lives and I hope I can help them grow as players, as individuals, in their spiritual walk, and just help them prepare for the next phase in their lives.

Coach Dillingham points out how connecting precedes coaching. Getting to know his players informs the coaching strategy he uses with each individual.

As a pitching coach, I felt that my personal connection with my pitchers was at least as important as the technical coaching I was providing. In my first year of college coaching, I made forming that connection my first priority. Being in my fifties at the time, I had children older than my pitchers, so my work was cut out for me being new to them ... and being old!

One of the first things I did was to institute a weekly "Pitcher's Lunch." This was held at an off-campus restaurant of their choosing with me gladly picking up the tab. We would meet up and enjoy a great lunch with no talk of softball. They were happy to get off campus and eat something other than cafeteria food, and I was happy to get to hang out with them away from the field (and bullpen).

It was at those lunches that a wonderful bond was formed that we still have today, years later. There I learned about their families, social lives, and future plans. More importantly, they saw my sincerity and that I was there with no agenda other than to build a friendship.

Chapter 1. Connecting Is Essential

J.J. Dillingham (left) with Sarah Vantrease, 2017 (photograph by the author).

Though I certainly fell short of the goal, my intention was to not only connect with my pitchers, but with every player on the team. If I couldn't connect, it wouldn't be for lack of trying. By connecting, bridges are built, walls torn down, and trust established. By putting forth the effort to connect, I was attempting to convey my love for each player, each in the way they dictated.

Because the need to connect with our players is ongoing, our efforts to maintain that connection must be ongoing as well. Knowledge of each player must continue, and that knowledge utilized to maintain the relationship.

A Big Ten All-Conference and All-Region shortstop captures how her coach connected with her, bringing her from an apprehensive freshman to an All-Great Lakes Region performer:

> When I first came to campus not knowing anyone I was anxious and excited. I did not know what to expect at the BIG 10 level especially how the program was going to be ran [sic]. My coach was a coach who really connected with me. She did not only connect with me on the softball level but on a personal one as well. The energy she brought everyday was contagious, she made me fall in love with the sport all over again. I found myself being excited to come to 6 a.m. lifts and being excited to get better and push my teammates. Looking back and

trying to pinpoint a way she connected with me is hard, it was not just one thing she did. Her contagious energy and the hard work she put in to push me is the main way she connected with me. She emphasized the importance of living in the moment and not taking any opportunity for granted. She allowed me to be myself while still pushing me to the next level and I am forever grateful to her.

We notice from her words that her coach did not employ a complicated strategy to reach her. Instead her coach connected in ways that were personal, consistent, and multifaceted. Her coach allowed her to be herself while motivating her to improve as a player and as an individual.

An outfielder from the same program sings the praises of this dynamic coach, who is all about connecting with her players:

One of my college coaches is my favorite coach of all time. Her love for softball put a smile on our entire teams' face every day. Her desire to win and her desire for us, as a team and individually, to do great things is unparalleled. She is goofy and fun and personable but knows how to compete and I think that balance is what makes her so easy to connect with. She also was able to be very real with me and I truly felt like I could talk to her about anything, especially softball related, and get a straight, honest answer. I always felt like she was in my corner and wanted the best for me. She is never afraid to dream big and set big goals and it is one of my favorite things about her. One of my biggest roles on the team was to elevate the group and my coach and I connected because we had those big goals in mind and we both wanted to share those desires with the team. The biggest factor that makes her an awesome coach is her love for the game and her love for our team.

One-on-one conversations are when we were able to connect the most. Whether that was in person, during or after practice and games, or over text. We were able to connect through softball on a real, person to person level and she was able to show how much she genuinely cared about me and the team and most importantly, how I feel and what my thoughts and ideas were.

She describes her coach as fun, personable, and even goofy, all means for this imaginative coach to connect with her athletes. Her coach connected by listening and loving. As this athlete shares, her coach cared about her and her teammates. She identified the most important element in the final sentence, that her coach cared about how she felt and thought.

This athlete's final sentence is instructive if we are to understand the differences between male and female athletes. Though having

Chapter 1. Connecting Is Essential

a coach who cares about them holds some importance to a male athlete, it is not an essential to play well or to win. Male athletes would be extremely unlikely to seek a coach who cares "how I feel and what my thoughts and ideas are." We would be wise to take note of this difference in outlook. Female athletes generally want and need a coach who cares on a personal level, listens, and conveys that they understand their player's thoughts and ideas. In short, they seek a strong connection with us as coaches, a bond that goes far beyond the field, bullpen, and weight room.

An All-Conference and former professional pitcher echoes what we are hearing from so many. She identified the way her coach connected on a personal, non-athletic basis. Once this connection was made and trust built, benefits were reaped on the field as well:

> My college coach is who I connected with hands down. Once I started playing showcase ball, he always seemed to find his way at my games. We quickly built a relationship, and not one that was based solely on softball. He got to know myself and my family and took the time to build those personal relationships. This played a huge decision in my choice to transfer there my last 2 years. Needless to say, he exceeded all expectations I had. The sense of family that was given when I played ball there was like no other. Between checking to make sure we were okay personally or checking in on our grades, I always knew he was there. This led to a bond and trust that we also shared on the field. This trust was even greater with being a pitcher. I knew that when he critiqued me or let me hold it that it was for a good purpose. We could always joke around and play, but we both knew when it was time to go to work. I can't say enough good things about him to be honest. I just hope he is still there when my kids are old enough to go to college!

A former PAC 12 Catcher of the Year and veteran of three World Series appearances speaks of connecting with three very different coaches in terms of personality and their way of connecting with her. All were effective in connecting and motivating her, though their styles varied widely:

> I connected with all three of my college coaches on different levels. They understood me in different ways, but all found their own special connection with me that pushed me towards tapping into my potential. My head coach was a man of few words—those words were often sarcastic or aggressive, but for me, it pushed me in a way that worked. He motivated me by way of tough love.
> It took me a lot longer to connect to one of my assistant coaches. I was

a stubborn player, especially in my early college years. I always wanted to know "why" and we butted heads some times because she wanted me to just do and ask later, but that wasn't the way I operated. We found, over time, that the more we communicated with one another, the better our relationship was and the better I performed because I was finally open to following her direction without friction.

My other assistant coach was the one I got along with the most from the beginning. He wanted to know me, who I really was to the core and he balanced the other two out really well. He knew when to jump me and demand more and also knew when to back off because I was beating myself up enough. This relationship is the one that has continued just as strong post-college. When one of my teammates passed away in a car accident, he called me to break the news. He's the first person to text me on my birthday (even before my parents) and the first on every holiday. This relationship, one that is fostered in truly understanding and caring for the individual as a person first and a player second, is the most important one I have.

A first team All-Conference catcher and NCAA Woman of the Year nominee speaks of the high respect level she had for her coach and how this formed the basis for her connection with him:

> My coach quickly earned my respect as I started my new journey as a collegiate softball player. He reached out prior to the season's start to provide welcoming arms to me and my family, resources, and opportunities. His willingness to continually communicate his thoughts, resources, and expertise while displaying patience is what strengthened my respect for him. He opened my eyes to new aspects of the game, especially the mental game. He included this aspect during all practices and games. His consistency in his actions made him someone who I could trust. The expectation of a hard work ethic in me as a student athlete seemed achievable since he in return displayed hard work and sacrifices for the team. (He worked a full-time job, drove an hour one way every day to practice/games, and stayed late to work through difficulties his players were having.) His willingness and patience to work through the small things with me individually improved my connection and appreciation of my coach. Because of the connection we built during these practice moments, he knew who I was as a player and a person and I knew who I had as my coach. This strengthened the connection, respect, communication, trust and success my team and I had for him.

We can observe that in one paragraph this player used the word "respect" three times to describe her feelings for him. She described his

Chapter 1. Connecting Is Essential

consistency, sacrifice, willingness, patience, and hard work. With these attributes as a foundation, this admirable coach was able to build a connection, one built not on words but on his very character.

An All-Conference outfielder cites her coach's interest in her past and future life as well as his ability to listen as factors that led to a strong connection: "Coach connected with me by being genuinely interested in my life. He cared about my past and wanted the very best for my future. He was very passionate about being a great role model so that I would strive to be a better version of myself. By listening so intently he became a leader in my eyes."

Despite our best efforts, there will be times and circumstances that strain our relationship with some of our players. As in marriage, friendship, and virtually every relationship, there will be friction and disagreement at times. Like any good relationship, the one between player and coach may not be all roses, and there will be rough spots where you might not even like each other very much. In spite of the challenges, however, the connection must be protected. The strong foundation of connection between coach and player is what allows for healthy disagreement or the airing of differences. In the end, if a meaningful connection is established and maintained, these storms can and will be weathered.

You may be reading all this information about connecting with a bit of frustration. It may be that you are just not a "connector." Engaging with people generally is just not something that comes naturally; in fact, you would rather not connect with people at all. If this is the case—change. Get help. Get some honest feedback from those close to you and begin to reach out to your players. Your success depends on it.

If we as coaches can't motivate ourselves to reach out to our players, our programs will never enjoy sustainable success. We may have a season now and then where we have a strong contender, but it will be built on talent alone, talent that is not maximized. To get the most out of our players on the field, we need to be all about connecting with them off the field.

This is one of the ways that coaching females demands more of a coach compared to males. It is not enough to recruit well and be a knowledgeable of the particular sport. It takes effort to reach and connect with female athletes, and sincerity and genuine concern must accompany that effort.

Chapter 2

Must They Love Their Teammates?

While having a team of female athletes who love each other would be ideal, this is a difficult goal to reach, and one that is probably a rarity. If we can foster blanket love between our athletes, there is no doubt that this dynamic will only make our team better.

Brandon Elliot, Head Coach of NCAA 2017 and 2018 Division III National Champions Virginia Wesleyan, writes of the impact team love had on his team's 2017 season:

> In 2016 we entered the NCAA tournament ranked #1 in the Nation and full of confidence. With two top tier pitchers and a few All-Americans, this was the year. We went two and out. In the regional. At home. We, I, were devastated, surprised, depressed ... embarrassed. Little did I know then, this was the best thing that could have ever happened to our program. Instead of riding the rest of the regional tournament out at home, in my self pity, I decided to join the grounds crew and in doing so, I was there, first hand when an "underdog" won the regional championship a few days later on our field. What I realized, in their moment of celebration, was what I, we, our program was missing.
>
> You see, we pride ourselves in our work ethic. We are blessed with a program full of a lot of talent and I feel, as a whole, we have an exceptional coaching staff. With all of that said I could really sit back and say we get out worked, out played or even out coached. But, in the biggest moments we were simply getting out loved. Now, don't get me wrong, we have always had a strong foundation of love in our program. However, we loved with boundaries. Fortunately for the future of our program, that was about to change.
>
> Fast forward through a few "team builders" and deep "conversations" about love and being out loved in the game's biggest moments and a group of kids came up with #OUTLOVE and a movement, for our program, was born. Simply put, outlove doesn't just stop at loving

Chapter 2. Must They Love Their Teammates?

others more than yourself. For our players it means loving each other in moments where the other person didn't deserve it. It means cheering for that teammate who plays over you even though you worked your tail off for that spot. It means trying to find a way to love "coach" when he is drilling the team. It means loving without boundaries and when you love without boundaries ... everyone feels value.

So, how did the year turn out, you ask? We went 54–3 and went on to win the NCAA DIII National Championship. To be honest, the impact of #OUTLOVE to that 2017 team can never be explained. It could only be felt.

For that team in that season under Coach Elliot's leadership, love for each other was a big factor in their success.

Brandon Elliot (left) high-fiving Theresa Cardamone with an unidentified fan in the background, 2017.

Coaching Women's Softball

Baylor Head Coach Glenn Moore is one of the most respected voices in college softball. Now in his twentieth year at Baylor with nearly nine hundred wins as a Division I head coach, he tells of the positive impact love between teammates can have:

> With over 30 years of coaching experience I've had many different types of teams. The dynamics change every year. Even if you graduate no one everyone will be a year older and the product of the previous year's experiences. My experiences have shown me that the teams that care deeply for each other will certainly have better chemistry and maximize their performance. The 2 most successful teams I've coached, finishing in the Final 4 at the WCWS were not in the top 5 of my most talented teams. Love is a powerful emotion (1 Corinthians 13:13) and I like to think that love is a "verb," an action. If you love your team you will provide for them things they need to be successful emotionally, physically and spiritually and the same applies within the team. Can you win without love? Sure, but it's more difficult and certainly less fulfilling.

Texas Tyler Head Coach Mike Reed reflects on the impact of teammates loving each other can have on their life experience as a college softball player. With a record of 595–118 record in fifteen years at UT Tyler, he is tied for fourth place in the NCAA with an .824 winning percentage. Going beyond winning, Coach Reed recognizes that positive memories are created and lifelong relationships established by having a

Glenn Moore, 2020 (Baylor Photography).

Chapter 2. Must They Love Their Teammates?

close-knit team. He writes of how he took positive steps to insure that this goal went beyond simply words:

> Just like every other college in the country, there is a part of our recruiting tour on campus when we sit down and talk about the things that are important to our program. We talk about what their daily experience as a student will be, the academic rigor and opportunities, a typical day at practice and of course sprinkle in some talking points of big wins, and the excitement of excelling on the field. Like everyone, we try to paint the picture of what it would look like for them to be at our school, in our program and enjoying a successful student-athlete softball career. The very last thing we comment on, we point to a picture of a dog pile or team celebration picture and we tell them that those girls in that picture 5, 8 or 15 years ago, they don't remember their ERA, they don't remember their batting average, they don't remember how many stolen bases they had, but they remember that moment. They remember the team excitement for a victory they all worked side by side for. They don't look back and think about that random Wednesday practice that they really felt connected in the box, or that bullpen that nothing seemed to hit right and they worked until they fixed the issue. They will remember the road trips that they bonded on, the team camping trip or the team karaoke night on campus where the most shy freshman belted out Journey at the top of her lungs. They will remember their teammates, and the life long friends they connected to, who they met in college because of softball and now stand beside them at their weddings.
>
> We said this talk over and over and for the first few years of my coaching career I thought, it just happens naturally, its part of the ebb and flow of a 9 month year, fall to spring they grow together, transition together. It's natural. It just happens. It's just the personality of each team and how they connect. Some years better than others. We have all had teams that you felt that they just clicked, the right group together, the right personalities mixed, and those teams seemed to excel more on the field. And then we all have had teams with talent maybe above others but just didn't have the IT, the connection, not bad, just not IT.
>
> I started to ask myself if we think this is so important, we talk about it with every recruit we have on campus, then we must cultivate it and grow it just like we would grow every other necessary skill for success. We started doing more team dinners, cookouts, more camping trips, karaoke nights, anything that could get this group of people from all different backgrounds to have common links, to share joy together and have to work hard side by side and share experiences together. There is no doubt our teams that have found that connection, a true genuine love for their teammates, have been more successful.

Coaching Women's Softball

While having a team that truly loves one another is our goal, this formula is not easily duplicated. The interactions between different personalities don't always allow for the dynamic we want to see in this regard. Nonetheless, love between players is a goal worthy of our attention, but is it necessary to be successful?

Laura Berg, Head Coach at Oregon State University, offers her experience with a team that loved each other, and with one that did not. A four time All-American at Fresno State, Coach Berg is one of four women in the world to win an Olympic medal in softball in four Olympic Games. The USA Hall of Famer speaks of the necessity of team love from a depth of experience few have: "I don't believe this is absolutely a must. It's amazing when teammates do love each other. I've experienced both in my career. The 2004 Olympic Team I feel truly loved each other on and off the field. We traveled so much together that I feel it helped us grow together and trust, respect and love each other. The National Championship team that I was part of didn't really get along off the field. We respected each other and loved each other on the field but didn't really hang out with each other off the field."

Janae Shirley is the Head Coach at 2010 NCAA Division III National Champions East Texas Baptist University. The former NFCA National Coach of the Year questions whether expecting a large team of female athletes to love each other is realistic or necessary to be successful:

> Love. That's a big word. I think in coaching 20–30 female athletes, saying that they all need to LOVE

Mike Reed (center) with K.K. Stevens (left) and Lexi Ackroyd, 2017.

Chapter 2. Must They Love Their Teammates?

each other is an unrealistic expectation. There are so many challenges that have to overcome already. They are all raised differently, come from different backgrounds, have different tendencies, different strengths, different weaknesses and different personalities. It's hard enough getting them to get to know each other, much less telling them that they have to LOVE each other. Love can't be forced. Love can grow and it can be real, but you can't force it to happen. Respect however, that is something that is a choice and can be demanded. I tell my players all of the time that I understand that they will not all love or even like each other, but if they will respect the fact that they are their teammate and what that means, we can all be successful. What does that respect look like? Well it looks like this. You respect their ability on the field, respect where they come from, you respect them by not being rude to them, respecting them enough to follow the same rules that they are following. Respect comes outside of the team, it means not talking about them to other people, not sharing their fears or things that they have going on. Respect ... now that for me and my program is a must.

Laura Berg (left) with Lovie Lopez, 2019.

Given that most teams operate without wall-to-wall love between its players, the question is not whether team love is desirable, but can we win without it?

Coaching Women's Softball

Janae Shirley, 2020.

Unconditional love for her teammates is not something that resonates in the mind of all female athletes. For males, the appeal to love each other makes sense on one level, and it works. Legendary teams of the past like the Detroit Pistons and the Pittsburgh Steelers attributed their success to team love. Men have been binding together, entrusting their lives to each other since time began, fighting wars, hunting for food, and protecting their collective families. Men who fought together in battle a half century ago are still emotionally bound to each other. In short, male athletes may do their best when they are bonded to their team, when they love their teammates.

Many female athletes, on the other hand, find it difficult to bond to every single team member. Trusting and drawing close to the entire group is difficult, based on my observations and the ever-present "drama" that infects many women's teams. This basic difference is critical to grasp if we are to effectively motivate females. While loving each other would be ideal, female athletes can be resistant to our efforts to force the concept upon them. Emphasizing love for your teammates, basing their success on the level of devotion to one another may have worked in an ideal situation but is not necessarily something that can

Chapter 2. Must They Love Their Teammates?

be "coached up." The female athletes I have coached were not eager to "love" teammates who they actually didn't care for, and felt that they could win without that dynamic present.

Continually preaching "love thy teammates" can actually be counterproductive to some teams. By asking for something they may not be inclined to do, the chance of failure is high. They hear us telling them that the team's success depends upon everyone loving each other, yet they cannot achieve what we have presented as an essential goal. If we as coaches believe success isn't possible without "team love," our players may see themselves and their season as doomed because team love may not be what drives that particular team.

On the necessity of players loving one another, an All-Conference catcher is unequivocal: "I certainly don't think that this is necessary or even possible for females playing at the highest level especially.... However, it's important to treat each other with the upmost respect and continuous encouragement and affirmation. So no you don't have to love them. You just have to show you're committed to the team and that you respect them."

An All-Region pitcher weighs in: "This is a hard one. I don't think it is possible to love everyone you're on a team with 100% of the time. Would it help? Of course. But it's just not practical. I do think you have to have the ability to put differences aside and not let these differences affect your play and the common goal. I don't believe you can win a championship with a bunch of conflict and hate. But do you have to 'love' everyone? Maybe not."

An All-American first baseman has reservations about team love and points out how emphasizing it can be counterproductive:

> I don't believe loving all of your teammates is an important role in the success of a female team. Most coaches pressure their team to do this with required "bonding" but what they don't realize is that more time spent together typically causes unwanted drama and tension within the team. Mandatory bonding won't cause everyone to love each other. Honestly, I don't think loving your teammates is something that can be forced at all. Of course there will be some that you do love deeply, but there are others you just won't get along with. I believe this is true on any female team.

In a research survey, 38 percent of college softball players surveyed answered "True" to the statement: "Having players who have a strong desire to compete is more important than having players who love each other."

Considering the degree to which the "Love your teammates" mantra has been repeated across woman's athletics, this figure is surprisingly high. In spite of the fact that we have been preaching love as absolutely essential for several years, almost 40 percent of our players still don't buy it, believing that the desire to compete is a better metric. A follow-up statement read: "Teammates must love one another in order to win." Again, a big chunk of our players don't think so, with 40 percent finding that statement false. Many of our players have reservations about this theory, possibly because they have rarely seen it work.

Although loving all of their teammates can be difficult for the female athlete, competing comes naturally to them. Anyone who has coached women for any amount of time will understand what I am about to say. Female athletes love to compete. They hate, really hate to lose. They develop ill feelings for their opponents and take great pleasure in dominating and defeating them. Building upon "compete" is something that female athletes buy into.

I witnessed a college softball game between a "mid major," unranked Division I team and a major conference opponent ranked in the top ten nationally. The smaller school was overmatched and by the middle innings had fallen behind by several runs. A player for the bigger school, one of their power hitters, stepped into the batter's box. Before the pitcher could begin her windup, the batter stepped out of the box with one foot and began to interact with her dugout, laughing and clowning around. Being one-sided, the game may not have been important to the batter at that point, but it was to the mid-major team's pitcher. Asking for a time out, she motioned to the umpire that she wanted a new ball. When he called for the ball she was holding to be thrown to him, she reached back and rocketed the ball on a line, hitting the unsuspecting batter squarely on the helmet. There was a momentary hush, followed by a confused look on the umpire's face and a shocked look on the batter's face. The pitcher stood defiantly, glaring at the batter for just a second, then giving an innocent face to the umpire as to say, "Oops!" That pitcher, on that night, regardless of the score, was not going to be mocked or disrespected. She may not have won the game, but in her mind, she won. Female athletes hate to lose and refuse to be bullied or mocked.

I was recruiting at a high-level travel ball game where many blue chip recruits were competing. The game was well attended by college coaches, many of whom represented nationally ranked programs. A

Chapter 2. Must They Love Their Teammates?

good number were there to watch an outstanding pitcher in the circle for one of these talented and well-coached teams. In the top of the first inning, the pitcher struck out the first two batters, but the number three batter got on due to an infield error. The number four batter hit the second pitch deep over the center field fence, scoring two. I looked for a show of emotion from the pitcher but saw none. She stepped back in to the circle and struck out the number five hitter for the third out of the inning.

I watched the rest of the game as this pitcher, who was being scrutinized by some of the biggest name coaches in college softball, dominated her opponents. I was so struck by her resilience and competitiveness that I can still recall that she pitched a perfect game following that home run, striking out twelve. Her team rallied late in the game and won 3–2. She treated the early home run as if it never happened. Her competitiveness went into overdrive, making it a long game for the opposing team's lineup. I have witnessed displays of competitiveness such as this countless times. It is not the exception—it is the very culture of fastpitch softball, the very DNA of female athletes.

A former Baylor pitcher recalls a war in NCAA Regionals where she battled for 16 innings to get the win: "We made it to our first regional at Baylor. We were the hosting team and we wanted to badly to win the region. We played 16 innings and finally won the game 1–0."

The pitcher, 2004 NCAA

Cristin Vitek Wafer, 2004.

Coaching Women's Softball

Player of the Year finalist Cristin (Vitek) Wafer, humbly left out that she threw a three-hit shutout, setting an NCAA record with 28 strikeouts. She faced 56 batters in the contest and threw 185 pitches in the nearly four-hour game. I believe we would be hard pressed to find such a display of sheer competitiveness in all of sports.

Every softball coach could tell of examples of extreme competitiveness on the part of their players. I am reminded of a freshman pitcher I coached who was pitching in her first college contest. Though the game took place in our fall season and technically didn't count in the books, it counted for this young pitcher who stepped into a college circle for the very first time.

Our opponent was a very strong Division I mid-major team who was the perennial champion of their conference. For us as a Division III program, this was a great opportunity. On the strength of a great rise ball and a tricky change-up, our freshman pitcher kept our opponents off balance, and the score was tied 1–1 after six innings.

Sometime during the seventh inning, our freshman injured her back while delivering a pitch. What we didn't realize until later was that she fractured a lumbar vertebrae that night. She insisted she could finish the game, which she did.

That fractured vertebrae would be a constant problem for her for the entire four years of college. Being a riseball/dropball pitcher, she was heavily affected by the nagging injury, as it rendered her unable to throw either pitch.

In order for her to have a chance to pitch at the college level, she allowed me to change her into a curveball/change-up pitcher, as these were the only pitches she could manage without intense pain. By throwing her curveball with great accuracy and delivering a deceptive change-up at knee level, she had four great years in the circle. She was All-Conference every year with wins over some of the top Division III teams in the country. Though she lived with pain that was exacerbated by pitching, she trained, worked hard, and won.

Though we tried everything from physical therapy to chiropractic to massage therapy (including a mystical massage therapist known as the "Witch Doctor"), nothing helped. She got by on pure guts, driven by her hyper-competitive nature. Our team rallied behind her, inspired by her need to compete.

If we are able to harness the collective power of these naturally competitive athletes into a team that is working together, success is likely to follow. What the players on most teams have in common is not

Chapter 2. *Must They Love Their Teammates?*

love; it is the need to win. While love is preferable, in most cases with most teams, we settle for compete, a powerful force as well. Capitalize on this. Build on women's natural desire to compete and win and bring your team together over these dynamics. Ideally, they should be devoted to one another in love, but this is often not the case. They don't absolutely have to love one another, but what is essential is that they must come together with respect for their teammates, ready to compete and win.

An All-American first baseman speaks of a love the team needs to have in common: the love of the game of softball. Driven by the love of competing in the sport they have sacrificed so much for, they are forged into a team that wants to win at all costs:

> I just think that love is directed towards something else. The team doesn't bond over loving each other, but over loving the game itself. There is a mutual understanding when everyone walks out to play, and that is that they are all there because they love the game. With that being said, even if you do not love your teammates, you need to be able to put your differences aside on the field because when it comes time to play it is a team sport. Even if You personally do well, You can't win the game alone. You will have to trust your teammates to also do their part. The trust comes from leaving personal feelings off of the field and watching how skilled your teammate actually is. You know you can trust their athleticism and skill to help lead the team to success. Trust and mutual love of the game are two key components to success, but loving all of your teammates is something most individuals aren't able to do.

An All-Conference outfielder recalls the intensity of her team that won a conference championship:

> The fire that you feel in your heart, when you know that you are a part of something bigger than yourself, is overwhelmingly passionate. My team's motivation to win is what drove me to work my hardest, push myself, and give everything I had in every play. My team's success was always bigger than my own and when you have like minded individuals working together for a common goal then you become a force to reckon with. I have been blessed to have many memories to look back on that continue to spark that fire inside me and even as I write give me goosebumps thinking about them. Many of these moments feature my freshmen year of college and the championship season my team and my coaches shared.

Coaching Women's Softball

It was not love that drove this particular team, but the competitive "fire" that spread to both players and coaches.

You can almost feel the competitive fire as this former All-Conference pitcher and hitter recounts her experience playing in NCAA Super Regionals. She speaks of a team possessed with competitiveness and determination to win. Her team came together over the thirst to win, to survive to keep pursuing a dream:

> Surreal. That is the word I would use to describe the game against Oregon State in 2016. There are games that seemed to be blurred, but this game was different. I felt the life that our team carried within them. I felt the "want to" that each individual eagerly craved. I saw the passion in each player's eyes during that game. We were a family and, as a team, we were determined to leave it all on the field that year. For a team to go through so much adversity and STILL have one another's back was a blessing.
>
> It is rare to be a part of a team where every single player has "the will to want to." That softball team was special, from the seniors all the way down to the freshman. The thirst for competition was apparent to all who were present.
>
> Fourteen innings. That was how many innings we played against Oregon State. Fourteen innings of fight, hurt, and energy. I was surrounded by young women that were determined to put our program on the map. It was 2–0 in the top of the seventh inning, and our team knew that two runs was not enough to hold the Pac-12 team. Sure enough, the score was 2–2 in the bottom of the seventh inning. The game flipped, against our favor, in the twelfth inning 4–2. The response from our team was a dream come true; each girl amped up their energy and became eager to catch up and win. We realized how tired we were physically and mentally, but not one of us saw that as an excuse.
>
> Bottom of the twelfth inning, down by two runs; picture that. Try to feel the heart rate going faster than you can count. Your head spinning because you're trying to power through the tired, pounding headache from all of the yelling and cheering. The emotions behind the fact that this could be our last game together. Making the unshared decision that we refuse for this season to be over just yet. The main thing that I recall from this inning was hearing my teammates yell behind me, while I am up to bat with two outs, and two strikes on the count. It was empowering to know that every girl on our team was invested, ready to fight with me. We were willing to win and we knew that it took every single one of us. That is exactly what we did. In the bottom of the 14th inning, we used all of our will to put together five runs to go ahead and secure the win over Oregon State. It took our entire

Chapter 2. Must They Love Their Teammates?

family, competing every single pitch, inning, and at bat to win that game. Our family succeeded on the sole fact of our eagerness to compete for each other.

Instead of forcing love, seek to build more tangible virtues like loyalty, kindness, patience, integrity and self-sacrifice. These character traits support a competitive spirit across your team, while the concept of loving teammates may or may not sink in.

UAB Head Coach Joe Guthrie agrees: "I believe that there is an overemphasis on 'team love.' It comes from a good place but lacks a connection to undeniable core values of life ... integrity, discipline, gratitude, etc." He goes on to differentiate between the player motivated by love and the one motivated by the need to compete: "The best players in an organization always value compete over love. More players in the past few years have valued love over compete. Getting the player that values love over compete more competitive is one of the secrets to greatness."

The most competitive player I have ever coached was my youngest daughter. A standout travel ball and high school pitcher, her quiet rage burned against every opposing player, batter and coach. She took that fire with her to college where nobody ever had to remind her to compete. In the summer after her junior year in high school, our travel team was competing in a large, prestigious tournament in South Carolina with 64 teams participating. Fighting through game after game, we reached the finals where we faced an Atlanta team stacked with players committed to SEC and ACC programs. My daughter pitched the entire game, a war that was scoreless after 9 innings. In the bottom of the tenth with two outs, the other team's runner on second base attempted to steal third. As our catcher began her throw to third, it was apparent that their runner was going to be out "by a mile." But instead of finding its mark, the ball sailed over the third baseman's head and into the far corner of left field. The runner scored, game over. We finished second, which is nothing to be ashamed of given the level of competition and sheer number of teams.

My daughter looked down in silence as the tournament director handed out the second-place trophies. As our head coach added his congratulations during the post game meeting, she remained silent. We walked out in silence and got in the minivan for the 12-hour ride back to South Florida. She looked out of the side window, exhausted, but her face was still intense, angry, and stayed that way for 12 hours. About an hour into the trip I heard her window pop open. In the side mirror I saw something flying out the window. I knew what it was and didn't need to ask. It was the second-place trophy.

The most informative thing about this story is the responses I get from players I share it with. They will typically say that they can relate, that they would feel the same way and have in the past in similar situations. One responded matter-of-factly, "If you didn't finish first, you lost." Softball players identified with this off-the-chart display of competitiveness and found it inspiring. Instead of considering this behavior extreme, they accepted it as the norm.

A standout second baseman relates her memories of being a part of a great team, one that was characterized by competitiveness:

> My favorite team of all time was my sophomore year of college. It was one of the hardest years. The year prior we had 18 players. The next year, 8 of them transferred, we lost our head coach and assistant coach to another school, and our school was contemplating the idea of not having a softball program. Our team truly was one unit that year. But more than that, we were so darn competitive with each other that every single one of us was the best player we could be that year. I'm talking, top batting averages and beat the best teams, and easily at that.

Another player, an All-Conference third baseman, still vividly recalls the intensely competitive team she was a part of as they fought for a conference championship:

> In college my team wasn't eligible for post-season for the first two years due to changing divisions. When we finally got to compete, there was no trace of doubt that we could win it all ... until we got to the second championship game (double elimination). We were determined we could win, and while we were exhausted our spirit was not. Extra inning turned into extra inning as we fought to win the title of conference champs. What should've been the last out dragged on to bases loaded with the winning run on third base. Yet even as we faced the winning run, we were determined that we would have the final say—we were not coming in second best. We managed to hold the runners and get the final out; we had another chance to drive in the final stake. All we needed was one run. Looking into the eyes of our strongest hitter, nervous at the task at hand. First pitch, first swing ... conference champions!! With a home run we sealed our victory! We could've given up when errors loaded the bases; we could've given up and said

Chapter 2. Must They Love Their Teammates?

we gave it a good run ... but the work we put in, and the competitive nature we cultivated, our only option was to win.

That particular player, whom I had the privilege to coach, played an entire season with torn ankle tendons and a broken thumb, downplaying her injuries so that she could continue to start and compete. She knew that we had only nine players that first year we began coaching that team, and that we had nobody on the bench. The next year she broke her nose and upper jaw diving into the fence after a foul ball at third base. Her injuries never diminished her extreme competitive spirit.

Another incident in that initial season of coaching for me characterized the competitive spirit of that group of special athletes. The previous year the team had been easily swept at home in a four-game weekend series by the conference champions. As we traveled the ten hours in the bus to play them again, we did so not with eighteen players but with nine. Of the nine, most had not even been starters the previous year and had watched their team get humiliated from the bench. As we took the field for warm-ups, the other team oozed confidence. Though we were in second place (two games behind them in the conference standings), we would have to win three games in this four-game series to capture the championship as this was the last regular season weekend.

There was an extra measure of pre-game tension as perhaps the home team picked up on the confident body language our players were sporting. As we were about to begin the game, the opposing coach informed me that I would not be allowed to call pitches from outside the dugout. This created a hardship since the visitors' dugout was oriented in such a way that the catcher would not be able to clearly see my signals if I was restricted to inside the dugout. We as coaches used these shenanigans to inflame our team, further stoking their competitive fires.

When the fourth game ended the next day, we had taken three of four games ... with only nine players. Hard-fought battles, won pitch by pitch. The home team shuffled off the field like zombies in shock to the certain tongue-lashing that awaited them from their now humbled coach.

We returned to our bus where our exhausted team sat surprisingly quietly. As the home team filed past our bus, one of our pitchers begin to sing, just barely loud enough for them to hear, "We kicked your #!*#, we kicked your !#*#."

This display was not commendable as far as good sportsmanship goes, but I found it instructive in understanding the female athlete's competitive spirit. It was not quite enough that her team won the series and stole the conference championship. She wanted to take one last shot, one last opportunity to remind them of who ended up on top. We won; you lost. Deal with it.

I believe what we are hearing from the players and coaches, and is born out by observation, is that our players unite more readily over competition than love. This is their common ground, their common goal: to compete and win. Love of teammates is certainly an admirable goal, if for no other reason that it minimizes team drama when people are forgiving, tolerant, and compassionate. We are most fortunate if we are able to experience a team where love abounds, but for most teams, players come together for one purpose: to compete.

Chapter 3

Loving Your Players

"Getting to know your players may be the most important thing you can do and letting your players know that you truly care about them, on and off the field. This will help you gain their respect and hopefully they will follow you in the trenches," says Ben Tyree, long time head coach at Trevecca Nazarene University.

This is a bold statement coming from a successful veteran with decades of coaching experience under his belt. Coach Tyree rates getting to know players and communicating that we care about them higher than all else. In his opinion, love for our players is the foundation on which great programs are built.

Although love between teammates may be less important to female athletes compared to males, receiving love from their coach is critically important to their success. Though the coach may be demanding and strict, as long as the particular style of the coach is delivered with genuine love, the female athlete will generally respond. Harshness, sarcasm, condescension, and plain meanness on the part of the coach, on the other hand, is extremely counterproductive to long-term success. A family atmosphere complete with fairness, authenticity, and sincere love and concern is where female athletes flourish. The effective coach combines this level of love with demands for discipline and a serious work ethic. Knowing there is a coach who loves and backs them allows the athlete to compete with minimal distracting player/coach drama.

Oregon State Head Coach and former U.S. Olympian Laura Berg explains the importance of loving her players:

> I feel it's essential for your players to know that you love them not only as softball players but at people too. They will run through a wall for you if they know you love and truly care about them. This is something I'm working on every day. Each and every athlete on the team (starters and non-starters) need to feel loved by their coaching staff. I meet with every athlete once a month to just catch up about things other

Coaching Women's Softball

Ben Tyree, 2019.

than softball. I want them to know that I care about them off the field just as much as on the field.

Keith Parr, long-time Head Coach at Christopher Newport University shares his thoughts on the necessity of loving his players:

> About a dozen years ago, I spoke to a group of high school coaches on the topic of motivating players. I did a lot of research in preparation for that topic, and the one thing that kept coming up was ... love! I spoke about that one word and elaborated about the power of that one word for the entire session. Good coaches care about their athletes as people. They sincerely want the best for their athletes in all aspects of their lives and are willing to help them in any way possible. They are invested and they take the time to get to know each of their players. If someone knows that you care for them, they are more inclined to be motivated to "buy in" to your program and ideas. Then the player will be more invested in the team and work hard to help the team be successful. Find ways within yourself to show how much you do love them in your own way.

Snead State Coach Tracy Grindrod connects loving our players with effective leadership: "Great leaders love and care about others more than themselves. Show that you care. Either you really love those you

Chapter 3. Loving Your Players

Keith Parr, 2019.

lead or you don't. If you don't feel it, don't fake it. People know when leaders are genuine and when they are not. There are many opportunities to serve those we lead, we just need to be aware and look for them."

What importance do our players place on our demonstration of love? Not surprisingly, 90 percent of players surveyed marked "True" to the statement: "I perform better for a coach who shows their love for me as a person."

The positive response underscores the female athlete's preference for a coach who is able to demonstrate love. They want and need our love if they are going to play to their full capacity. The responses to this survey question underscore the fact that our female athletes need the demonstration of love. In tangible ways we must be ready to meet this most critical need.

I believe they are also telling us that they need love that is articulated. This addresses what can be a core issue in coaching female athletes successfully.

We can adopt or even embrace loving our players as one of the primary foundations of our program, but if that love is buried in a purpose statement, it has no effect. As in any human relationship where love is present, it must be expressed verbally. Our players need to hear from us on a regular basis that we care about them. They need to hear from our mouth that they are valued, that they have a very special status with us.

When asked the follow-up question, "My coach loves me unconditionally and has my back," only 75 percent answered in the affirmative. While this is not as bad as it could be, we've got to do better. We have to wonder what is holding a good portion of us back from loving our players and being the person they can always depend upon. Determining why some coaches withhold love and loyalty goes beyond the scope of this discussion, but if you fall into this group, changes need to be made for your sake and the sake of your players. These young people who have chosen to play for us deserve to be loved. If you are unable to deliver in this area, get the help needed to grow and change. How tragic is it that some of us actually do love our players but are unable to express it. Athletes playing for this type of coach live with the conclusion that we don't love them.

A standout infielder sums up what defines a loving coach in her mind: "I have played for a handful of coaches that have loved me. They all have one thing in common: they care. They have all taken the time to build a personal connection with me and cared about my personal life outside of softball."

Love for our players encompasses not only the things we do for them; it frames what we do not do. It is love that can keep us from saying things to them in anger that should never be said. It is love that can drive out our impatience and lack of sensitivity. It is love that makes us hesitate a moment when we begin to lose our temper with a player. And it is love that brings us back to our core values of respect and selflessness.

Not surprisingly, the coaches I hear talking about loving their players are usually from very successful, perennial top tier college programs. The rest of us who toil in the other college programs, high school, and club teams need to grasp this essential ingredient. We need to learn from the successful coaches, not only their technical tips but how they sincerely love their players. These coaches are successful year after year in spite of different players rotating into the program and no matter whether dealing with millennials or generation Z. Their perpetual presence in the top 25 and being in post-season play traces back to the fact that these great coaches know how to love their players. Their teams reward them with the hard work and winning attitude that are necessary for success on the field.

Wisconsin Associate Head Coach and NPF (National Professional Fastpitch) veteran Danielle Zymkowitz speaks of how her success was fueled by the encouragement and love of her coaches and teammates.

Chapter 3. Loving Your Players

Following the example set by her coach, she formed her own coaching style, to "lead with love" as she puts it:

> When I finished my college career at the University of Illinois, I had no idea what I wanted to do as a career so I tried out for the Chicago Bandits, a professional softball team based out of Chicago. I made the team and had the opportunity to play in the NPF (National Professional Fastpitch) for 7 years, where the average a professional softball player career is about 2 years. As I was approaching the end of my playing career in 2017 and investing full time in my coaching career, I was doing a lot of reflection. How did I earn this opportunity to play for the same organization for 7 years? How was I able to juggle coaching, training and playing in the NPF for 7 years? How do I have three Championship rings for the Bandits? How did my coach and teammates become my best friends and such instrumental people in my life? How was I going to feel hanging up the cleats for the first time? It was all so surreal to me, this dream that I have been living playing professional softball. As the thoughts were all over the place in my head, one thing kept coming up. I had an owner, coach, and teammates that believed I could be something great. They saw something that I did not see. I was just a kid that just loved to play softball. They pushed me. They picked me up when I failed and they are still continuing to do that to this day. They loved me. For this, I will forever be grateful. I once heard a coach say "They don't care how much you know, unless they know how much you care." I swear by this quote. I would not be where I am today if I did not have coaches and teammates that believed in me and cared so much for me. They showed me by example and taught me what it was like to lead with love. I try every day to model my coaching after the coaches and teammates that mentored me and helped me accomplish things I never even dreamed of. So, thank you Bill Sokolis, Michael Steuerwald, Amber Patton, and Tammy Williams. I hope to keep leading the next generations of softball players the same way I was led by you.

A first baseman recalls the love of a travel ball coach that endured for a decade. This insightful coach rang all the bells when it came to loving this player. He expressed it, demanded excellence, and cared about her future outside of softball. He was loyal and not afraid to show emotion, being there for important milestones:

> I have had tons of coaches throughout my softball career, but the one who showed the most love to my teammates and me was probably my coach from 10–14u. I ended up going to middle and high school

Coaching Women's Softball

with his daughter so he was pretty much around for my entire softball career. This individual showed love by expressing it to all of his players. He would give me the biggest bear hugs, but would also set fear in my heart if I EVER struck out looking again lol. He knew when to be serious, take it easy, be a role model, goof off, and even discuss important decisions you may be facing. This man was around for 10 years of my softball journey. He was one of the first people who I cried on after playing my last high school game for the school I adored. Not only did he show love on the field, he wasn't afraid to show it off the field. Him and his family attended my graduation party and graduation. At the end of both of these events, he handed me a handwritten letter. It instantly put me into tears. It basically said how grateful he was that I played with his daughter for all those years and that he would always be on my side if I ever needed anything.

A former All-Conference Division I pitcher tells how her favorite coach showed his love for her: "He took an interest in me and my well being. He never over pressured me or made me feel like a failure if I didn't perform well. He always took time to be there for extra practice, and he cared enough about me to figure out the style of critiquing that worked for me."

An All-American shortstop and record holder for highest batting average in all of Division II speaks of the love her coach has for her entire team:

> Our coach is a living legend! Not only does he have over 400 wins, but he cares for his girls as if they were his own. I can't count how many times Coach would call me down to his office and just ask me how I was doing. There have been so many different situations where I have sprinted down the stairs to his office to tell him some big news, whether it be bad or good. He is a man who is easy to lean on. He is a parental figure for the team to look to while being away from home. He is also stern and makes you work for the things you get. He demonstrates love towards us by making us be the best we could be, and he initiated that relationship by being someone we could trust.

A Conference Player of the Year, this shortstop has a National Championship under her belt. She speaks of a coach who relies on actions as well as words. He shows that being loving and being tough go together perfectly:

> A coach I believed loved me was my college Head Coach. Although he displays his love a little bit differently, and one may not always take

Chapter 3. Loving Your Players

Danielle Zymkowitz, 2019.

what he has to say as being "loving," but he truly does love each one of his players. In my four years playing for him, my first two years were rough (especially that first year). I felt that he critiqued every little thing I did and was always expecting perfection from an imperfect person. What I didn't realize those first two years that I realized in my last was that he was teaching me some valuable life lessons, helping develop my character and resiliency, and preparing me for the real world. He's tough because he loves each of us. He's tough because he truly cares. He loved me enough to care to bring out the strong woman that I didn't know was in me.

Love like this coach demonstrated is powerful. This player attributes her transformation into a strong woman to his purposeful love.

A teammate echoes the impact of her coach's tough love, a love that was characterized by doing:

He's one of those coaches that expresses "tough love," but love nonetheless. He showed us that love by his high expectations for us on and off the field. He knew of our capabilities and potential, even if we didn't. He pushed us because he loved us. Even if it was hard for us to acknowledge that sometimes.

There's no doubt that Coach is a competitor, as are his players. But his passion went beyond the field. As a father of 3, he cared for each and everyone of us as if we were his own. He really went above and beyond for us without expecting much in return. He would cook us all dinner from time to time, send us encouraging/uplifting texts every now and then, come and help us when we had car trouble (which happened quite a few times), but above all of that, we ALWAYS knew his office door was open to us. He loved it when we came in to just talk, even if it wasn't about softball. Each and every one of his players knows, if we needed help, advice, to vent, or whatever else, we could always come to him. His love was portrayed not necessarily by what he said (especially on the field), but rather by what he did for us.

As a player who spent time at three different colleges, this catcher/3b has seen her share of coaching styles. She raves about the love she received from the entire coaching staff at her final school. She speaks as one who has been a part of a National Championship:

As someone who played at 3 different colleges, I can attest to the fact that there are many different coaching styles out there. Some styles can be laid back, some strict, some in between, but I can tell you one thing, not all styles show you love. Whole-hearted, genuine love and that is what I experienced. My experience with my travel ball team under was very similar to my college team, but when you are in college on your own, having a coaching staff that you know genuinely cares for you and shows you real love, changes your entire college experience. Our entire coaching staff showed us love on the daily, from them straight up saying "love you, kid," to jokes, to the fights in between, you knew at any second you could count on them to be there for you. I knew at any second I could call any of the coaches and they would be there for whatever was needed. No questions asked. Every person has a unique way of expressing love and it never had to be actually said. You just knew. From the second I stepped on the campus, I knew I was loved and I knew I had people in my corner for life. To this day, I know I can pick up the phone and call any one of those coaches and they would still be there. No questions asked. If that doesn't show true love, I'm not sure what does. This softball and coaching staff is something special.

This All-Region designated hitter provides this thoughtful summary of the ways her coach loved his players. Looking beyond their careers as athletes, he used his position to develop them into mature women who were prepared to meet the challenges that lay ahead:

I played four years of collegiate softball at under Coach. From the outside looking in, most would say he is "rough around the edges." Coach

Chapter 3. Loving Your Players

is firey, competitive and determined to win. When you are on the softball field it is always business. He is what most would describe as a "tough" coach, but it is the competitive environment that allowed our team to flourish. We were challenged and pushed allowing us to break through our glass ceiling and win championships. I loved the competitive environment. But after playing for Coach for four years and having the opportunity to be a graduate assistant, I was able to learn the other side of Coach and the love he has for his athletes. He builds a family culture outside of the field that translates to the field and contributes to the foundation of a winning culture.

When you were on the field you were expected to give 110% and perform to your highest ability. You were pushed to be the very best you can be. After my playing career I was able to become a stronger person able to handle failure and adversity. I was able to handle criticism and the truth, even when it was hard to hear. I could not be more thankful for this. After being in the workforce for two years, I have noticed that my experience in a competitive college athletic environment has propelled me past my colleagues in being able to handle stressful situations and feedback. To me, the competitive environment created by Coach that helps to shape his athletes into successful, productive members of society is one way he demonstrates his love. He helps to mold you into a better person in preparation for your life after college athletics.

Outside of the softball field Coach was a like a second father figure to his players. No matter what issue you were having or what you needed to talk through, he would make himself available. He would have given us the shirt off his back if we needed it. He constantly made sure we had what we needed. While he may have been hard on us on the field, he was always there for us for whatever we were going through. I think this is one of the most important values he provides to his athletes. The years an athlete is in college are often full of new experiences and struggles as you are learning to be an adult away from your family. Having a mentor to be there for you helps to navigate these waters more smoothly. Additionally, he constantly encourages his players to treat one another as family. We are taught to respect one another. When you in charge of many young women together, naturally there tends to be conflict. But Coach constantly encouraged forgiveness and respect, building the family culture within the team. This is Coach's second way of showing his love for his athletes.

It is interesting that this athlete equated being pushed and challenged on the field with love. She saw this tough behavior as being an aspect of his love and commitment to prepare them for life. Another All-Region player from this program echoes this understanding:

Coaching Women's Softball

Throughout my first 12 years of being a competitive softball athlete, I was coached by several different individuals who taught me what it meant to compete. Not only did they teach how to compete, but more importantly they taught me what it meant to be a better athlete and teammate than I was yesterday. They instilled in me the values of work ethic, self motivation, and the importance of optimistically accepting constructive criticism. With that said, in the process of looking to further my softball career in higher education and to find a new place to call home for the next four years, finding a coach who embraced these qualities was of the utmost importance to me. I found all these qualities in this coach and so much more. He demonstrated his love for us by pushing us as competitors on and off the field. He was available to us not just as our coach, but also as a mentor. His "open door policy" allowed us to reach out when we needed help outside of softball. This proved that we were loved beyond the talents we possessed on the field.

A conference Woman of the Year, NCAA Academic All-American of the Year, and NCAA Woman of the Year finalist spoke of the love in action her coach demonstrated and the impact this had on her life:

> My head coach loved his players. There is no doubt about that. He told us he did multiple times, but his actions always spoke louder than his words. He wanted to be involved in our lives, on and off the field, because he really did care about each and every one of us. He meant it when he said that he wanted to be the first person we called if something happened or we needed a ride. Coach genuinely cared about our well-being as people, not just players on a softball team. If someone experienced a loss, Coach was there and would make sure the team knew and was supportive. If someone was having financial issues, Coach would find an on-campus job. If someone was having trouble in school, Coach would find ways to help through tutoring or allowing time to go to mentoring sessions. As I reflect back, it is so apparent that Coach went above and beyond for us in all of these instances out of compassion. He planned team meals and team gatherings because he knew the secret to any successful team was team cohesiveness. He also allowed the team to be involved with his life and invited us to spend time with his family. This meant a lot to us since we were away from our families and it showed that he trusted us.
>
> We always said that our softball team was a big family, from the coaches, to the players and all the player's family members. This is not something that just happens organically and not every team has the joy of getting to experience something this special. I believe that

Chapter 3. Loving Your Players

this familial atmosphere came to be because of the values that Coach incorporated into the team through his coaching and caring. We were in it together and everyone mattered. I will forever be thankful for the love that Coach Wilson showed me when I was a player and the love he continues to show me now. He has made a lasting impact on my life and I will always respect and love him as well.

A JUCO All-American outfielder speaks of a coach who was intentional about loving his players and earned their love by his thoughtful actions:

> My respect for my JUCO coach started before I even met him—hearsay from players before me. He had a good reputation in the softball community. It didn't take long to understand for myself what kind of man and coach he was. He was open to us about his love for God and his family, and he treated each of us like his own. In doing so, I grew to respect him as I would my own parent. His expectations of me were clear both on and off the field. He was a coach I cared to make proud and tried not to disappoint. Not every coach earns that level of respect from their player, but Coach was definitely one for me.
>
> I learned as many (or more) life lessons from him as I did softball lessons. He emphasized the importance of studies first, softball second. He taught us to be strong, independent women. He empowered us to see our value and frequently spoke to our individual strengths in order to build us up. He met each player right where they were. He got to know us on a personal level in order to know our needs. Some needed tough love and a loud voice to get motivated. Others, like myself, needed words of affirmation and a pat on the back to get motivated.

It is no coincidence that this team was the 2008 JUCO National Champions and 2009 runner up. Notice the active verbs used to describe the love of this coach. She uses words like "empowered," "taught," "spoke to our strengths," and "got to know us to know our needs." This is the type of love in action that we would be wise to emulate.

A PAC 12 All-Region infielder felt the love of her coach through his faithfulness while she was recovering from elbow surgery. His words of encouragement hit home because of his genuine concern for her during that challenging time:

> I can't quite put a finger on a specific instance or action, but I remember how much it meant to me to have my coach's support after I had undergone Tommy John surgery. The most memorable act of

appreciation and praise I felt from him was his patience and willingness to work with me while recovering from the surgery as well as words of affirmation that he would sprinkle in as I had progressed. Many athletes understand how strange it is to go through injuries, big or small, and to have a coach who is patient and willing to work with you is huge. I felt appreciated through his constancy to try to help me be the best I could be through the high and lows.

A Division I pitcher relates her memory of a travel ball coach, "Benny," whose love meant everything to her and her team:

> He used to call us "his girls" and that he'd adopt every one of us without hesitation because he loved us like his own. Not a single team member doubted that. We were closer as a team because of his love for us. We respected him and each other and the concept of our team as a whole because of his love. One day we all arrived for practice, and Coach Benny had us all load up in his truck and we went for ice cream instead of practicing. We all thought it was the coolest thing. The next day I learned that Coach Benny had been diagnosed with cancer, and he had found out the news before scheduled practice the day before. Instead of cancelling practice, instead of telling us, he had just wanted one last time with "his girls" with everything happy and normal. He wanted to watch us laugh and be a team family one more time before he shared news that would change things. Coach Benny kept coaching us for as long as he could while being treated. When we reached high school ball, he didn't miss a game until his body physically wouldn't allow him to be there anymore. When Coach Benny passed, our group went separate ways. No one was able to coach our team like he was able to. He truly loved each of us, we all knew it, and we played differently because of it.

This is the impact a coach who is willing to love their players can make.

Lipscomb University Assistant J.J. Dillingham speaks of a love for his players that extends far past their playing careers:

> I hope the players that I come in contact with know that I love them more than just softball players. I care about them as individuals and I want to know what's going on in their lives. It's so awesome to watch your players grow in different areas while they are with you and I hope that I have had some positive impact on their lives. But it doesn't just stop when they graduate or leave our program. I want to know when things are going well so I can celebrate with them, but I also want to know when things aren't going so well and hope that I can help during those times, whether it's a hug or just to be there to listen. I have been

Chapter 3. Loving Your Players

honored to perform four weddings for former players and I have baptized two of our players. Being asked to be a part of special occasions like these are more important to me than any championship I could be a part of.

Birmingham Southern College Head Coach and former Auburn standout Kimball Cassady reflects on her high school and travel ball playing days under longtime University of Alabama Huntsville Coach Les Studeman:

> We all knew she loved us because of the way she pushed us to be our best. She really got to know us on a personal level and even when she would raise her voice, you might hate her to death at that moment, but you still wanted to be the best for her. To this day, she still keeps in touch with a lot of us. She was an open book if there ever was one. She had no problem telling you how she felt about you, the situation, the play or whatever it may be, but she always did a good job of letting you know after the fact that she loved you, but she knew that we could be better.

Coach Cassady's experience highlights the fact that love doesn't have to be delivered in any particular way; it just has to be delivered. Our personalities obviously differ greatly and we express love in different

Kimball Casady, 2017.

ways. Loving our players doesn't mean that we have to reinvent ourselves as Mr. Rogers. Be authentic and be yourself, but make sure that you intentionally demonstrate and verbalize your love to the players on your team.

A standout second baseman tells of how she was affected by the love of an assistant coach: "I had an assistant coach in college that cared about more than just softball. I think that was the moment I knew he was one of the best coaches. He demonstrated how much he loved our team and us individually because he knew what music we all liked, he knew our parents, he asked us questions about our life, he cracked jokes. He cared about more than my batting average and at what spot in the lineup I should be. Simply put, he just cared about all of me."

Perhaps a quality head coaches should look for in an assistant is whether he or she can love players. An assistant coach can supplement the head coach in that area and should be able to draw closer to some players than someone in the head coach role. An All-Conference outfielder speaks of how an assistant coach communicated his love to the team:

> During my playing years in college, our assistant coach was such a steady and consistent figure to balance our head coach, and I think this balance was essential to the success of our team. Apart from that, the support this coach gave each and every player throughout the years was unconditional. Every day before practice he would have a silly question of the day for our team; I always felt as though it was meant to bring light-heartedness and relief to our stressful lives, and I could tell this was a way he showed he cared about us more than just winning. This coach always made it a point to ask me how I was doing and showed a genuine interest in me and my life.

An All-Region Pitcher tells of her relationship with her coach: "This coach would go above and beyond to talk with us, check in on us, ask us questions about what was going on with us and share stuff about himself to build that connection that showed how he really cared more about us than he did about softball." The final sentence spoken by this player captures what this kind of love looks like to a player. This coach "really cared more about us than he did about softball." If our concern for our players is conditional, based on what goes on between the foul lines, we have missed the boat entirely. True love is when we care about the whole person regardless of her performance, and our players know this kind of real love when they see it. The love this player spoke of was

Chapter 3. Loving Your Players

demonstrated by her coach's willingness to engage with her as a person and not a player. This is love that takes the effort necessary to find out what is going on in the life of the player and to engage over areas other than softball. Walking the fine line between conversation and prying, we gather information from her and bring these subjects up to show we are cognizant of the forces present in her life.

The term "Tough Love" may have been overused, but this is a necessary component of the love we seek to give our players. We are the ones who must take the long view, doing what perhaps nobody has ever done in the life of a player, things like setting boundaries and limitations on behavior. Love means enforcing rules and dispensing discipline where necessary, even if our athlete is totally unaccustomed to such leadership and love. When we demand compliance, when we push against laziness, selfishness or arrogance, we are loving our players and should not step off from the challenge. Real love sometimes means taking a hard line because you care about your athletes' future as human beings.

Arizona State Assistant Coach Jimmy Kolaitis speaks of the responsibility of the coach to exercise this type of love with his or her players: "I do think we tend to fail in an athlete's development sometimes, because in today's society we are expected to baby them and tell them that everything is going to be ok. There is a time when we show our care for our athletes through being tough on them. We must be stern in our teachings, hold them accountable to expectations and standards. Tough love is showing them that we care. Sometimes they may not see it right away, but for the most part they will appreciate it later in life."

We should not make the mistake of thinking that the love we show players will always return to us. The most unlovable among our players, those who extract the most effort from us, are the very ones who find it difficult to love us back. Don't be surprised if your efforts to love some players are misconstrued, turned on you, and you are rewarded with wrath and disloyalty. We had an outstanding player who was particularly difficult to love. Manipulative, divisive, and calculating, she sowed discord on the team and tried to rally the team against the coaches. Ever the victim, her tears flowed easily. Knowing her dysfunctional family dynamic, we put extra effort into loving her and supporting her on the field and off. Eventually she had one of her many meltdowns during a game. My final encounter with her involved both her and her father hurling loud verbal abuse at me and her father wanting to engage me in a fight. My last memory of the two of them was the Campus Police escorting her dad off campus and the player spewing out insults at me.

Coaching Women's Softball

Unfortunately, she had to be removed from the team at that point. The incident reminded me that sometimes those who extract the most love from us give the least back.

We loved and supported another player through personal difficulties that included being a domestic violence victim and possible drug abuser. Her troubles started when she was accused of cheating in one of her classes and was suspended from playing for a season. Whenever a new issue appeared, we loved. If discipline was warranted, we administered it, but mostly we loved and guided her through a rocky time. This player too eventually had a meltdown, blaming the coaches for her shortcomings on the field and for losing out in the conference championships. She later assaulted a teammate and was subsequently banned from campus.

These examples shouldn't dissuade us from our responsibility to love our players. Every coach could add similar stories to the two I recounted. Some players will return the love, some will not. Loving them has value in and of itself. Their response is not the issue.

Loving our players is a difficult assignment. Janae Shirley, Head Coach at East Texas Baptist University, speaks about her journey in this area and how she grew into a more loving coach:

> For me, my coaching philosophy and purpose has drastically changed over the years. Early in my career I was very much driven to win and ultimately that was my only objective. What my players got out of our program or out of playing wasn't really a thought that crossed my mind. I was selfish and it was all about me and what they could do for me. It took really understanding my calling and my own purpose to understand that caring and loving for my players was my purpose, not just winning. I truly believe that every coach has their own way of showing their players that they love them. For me, how I show my players I love them is simple: I expect and demand their best and am not satisfied with anything less. I want them to not only be good softball players and grow in that area, but I want them to be equipped to be able to handle any situation that comes at them later in life. I want them to be successful. You see for me, loving them means allowing them and pushing them to be their best self. Typically its not fun for them at the time, but it's later they know and realize that I did those things because I love them.

What worked for her in terms of personality and demeanor will differ from other coaches. The love is the same, but the expression of it differs. Coach Shirley attributes her transformation to the words of a fellow

Chapter 3. Loving Your Players

coach. Taking cues from one of the best, she was motivated to get more serious about loving her players:

> I truly believe that players want to be pushed and want to be held accountable, but they do need to see that you love them. Forever it was hard for me to be able to show them that and get them to understand that. I had the opportunity to hear Patrick Murphy (University of Alabama Head Coach) speak one time. During his talk, he went on to talk about affirmation that they did in their program and what they did for their team and for each other. The growth that it allowed them to have. Listening to him made me realize that sometimes, just saying what you love about a player to them or in front of them allows them to see that.

Coach Shirley did more than think about how to love her players. Motivated to make changes for the better, she put new activities in place to change the culture and provide a place where love could be expressed:

> That year, we started something new. We called it the "hot seat." We would do the hot seat before team meetings or bible studies. I would basically pick one or two players each time and sit them in the middle of the team. I would then randomly pick 2–3 players on the team to affirm them. They needed to understand that the affirmations were not about their ability or their outward appearance, but about their soul and about them as a person. Once the players affirmed them, then it was my turn. I was shocked; by me actually saying those things to them in front of their team, those girls would get emotional and be shocked. You see for them, they thought that because I was tough on them and pushed them, I didn't like them. In reality though, I did those things because I did love them, but me saying out loud allowed them to believe that.

What Coach Shirley did deserves closer attention. Not only did she create a forum of transparency where love between teammates could be expressed, she was all in as well. Such openness showed her players that behind their coach was a person, a person who had noticed them and even loved them. For most of us as coaches, this type of self-disclosure is way outside of our comfort zone. Yet this insightful coach changed how she thought and found a way to give her players the love they needed.

Much of coaching is correcting. We spend the bulk of our practice time correcting technique and pointing out mechanical errors. This is necessary, but depending on how it is delivered, can inhibit a player's progress rather than to elevate their game. Yet these corrective messages, these lessons absolutely must be delivered. When we have laid

Coaching Women's Softball

a foundation of love and transparent concern, our players are more inclined to heed our instruction and make needed changes. Without the backdrop of love, instruction can be misconstrued as criticism and disapproval. When they feel cared about as a person, they are secure enough to accept instruction and make changes.

Though we all may strive to love our players, the greatest obstacle is often ourselves. A great coach I teamed up with had a heart of gold and genuinely loved our players. He was a religious man who viewed coaching as a calling. Watching him with the team, his concern for each player was unmistakable. He had one problem, however, and that was his temper. Though he never cursed, his anger was easily riled and could be explosive. This trait negated the very real love he endeavored to coach with. When he railed at one player over a minor issue, the whole team took his words to heart. An apology worked the first time, but unfortunately the displays of anger continued. After watching him for two years, I would say that he failed to impact his players in the way that he purposed and had lost the opportunity to show them the real love he felt for them.

A bad temper is not the only love killer. Besides the obvious behaviors that inhibit love in any relationship, seemingly small things like failing to listen when players speak to us, inappropriate sarcasm, and embarrassing them will undo our best efforts to love.

A lack of concern for a player's legitimate need for special attention is another way to lose her. I recruited a very talented outfielder for over a year. Although I coached at an NCAA Division III college, it was my goal to draw players who could compete at the Division I level. This outfielder was such a player. While we were able to get her on campus for an official visit, ultimately she accepted a scholarship at a Division I university.

During the Christmas break of this player's freshman year at the Division I school, I received a call from her travel ball coach. He told me that she had had quit her new team after the fall season and withdrawn from the university. She wanted to work the rest of the school year then come play at my college starting the next fall if we would have her. I told him of course but wanted to know the background of her leaving that school. I couldn't imagine there being an attitude or work ethic issue with this kid. She was as hardworking and respectful as they come. I knew her travel ball and high school coaches well, and they both raved about her character.

What I eventually learned was that her coaches, who were in

Chapter 3. Loving Your Players

their inaugural season at that university, were totally uninterested and unsympathetic to the fact that this girl had type 1 diabetes. This is the serious, insulin dependent, potentially fatal type of diabetes. The player was completely functional but needed the coaches to be aware of what to look for if an episode occurred. She wasn't asking for special treatment; in fact she went on to be one of the hardest working and most fit players on our team. Her coaches made the issue hers alone and refused to become informed of how to recognize danger signs. This total lack of concern for her health, maybe even her life, was unacceptable to her. She couldn't play for coaches who had no love for her as a person.

This player went on to be a four-time All-Conference outfielder for us. We kept an eye on her during practice and games, and other than giving her some juice or candy to balance her sugar level now and then, it was never an issue. Her first college coaches couldn't be bothered with her health issue, so she decided that she couldn't be bothered with them. Not surprisingly, those coaches were unsuccessful in their short tenure at that Division I program, moving on in just a couple of years.

The power of love to bring a player on board or to "buy in," as we coaches like to say, is hard to overestimate. An example from my days as a Federal ATF Special Agent shows how drastic changes happen in people who feel loved.

I was investigating the criminal activities of the local chapter of a violent street gang. I had partnered with a Fort Lauderdale, Florida, detective who was the local street gang expert. As we opened the investigation, progress was slow, as was typical of investigations of close-knit groups like these. One day we found out that the leader of the gang had been arrested on minor charges and was in the county jail. As we sat in an interview room with him, we asked him about himself and his family. A relationship began to develop between him and the detective and myself. Looking beyond the violent criminal that he was, we both saw a person who longed for a father figure. Perhaps the fact that the detective and I were in our late forties and the leader was about twenty years old played into his attachment to us as father figures.

That gang leader unexpectedly became an informant for us, providing a load of information about crimes past and present, membership, leadership structure, and connections with other criminal organizations. He did so without any help from us with his charges and without being paid. He turned on his gang brothers for us and introduced an undercover agent into the group. He effectively brought down the entire organization single-handedly. Why he did this for us puzzled the detective and me at the time but came to light later.

Just after the case ended, we tried to help the now former gang leader to start a new life. At his request we arranged for him to apprentice at a trade by calling in a favor. We helped him get set up in an apartment and encouraged him to embark on a new path. About a year later, the leader predictably became involved in criminal activity again and was sentenced to a lengthy prison sentence. It was then that I received a letter at my office from him. In that letter he told me how much our relationship meant to him. He wrote of how from our first meeting he saw genuine love from the detective and from me. Not knowing his father, he said he considered both of us to be his father. He was ashamed that he got involved with crime again, and he knew he let us down. Finally, he thanked me for my friendship and for being the role model he needed to help him make good decisions in the future. I still have that letter over twenty years later.

In short, that criminal cooperated with us (law enforcement) for no other reason than he felt loved by us. Imagine the impact love could have on our players.

Huntingdon College Head Coach Casey Chrietzberg tells of her journey from being a task-oriented X's and O's coach to one who embraced loving her players as her first priority:

> My title is "Head Softball Coach" but I have come to realize that portion of my job is actually what I feel I do the least. This year, more than ever, I have put more time into each of my players than ever before. Both them individually and them as a team doing "non softball" related events. This year we had a bigger incoming class than we had returners. I found out we had a "team health" problem this year in January, literally a couple hours before the first spring practice. At first upon hearing the news I was mad, but after taking some time to think on it, I recognized I had created a recipe for this to happen and did not use our fall well enough to mesh the team together. I could not blame the team for not taking the time to do something I myself did not show them first.

I know from coaching against Casey both at Huntingdon and while she coached at Emory University that she is a very competent, hard-working, successful coach. Her emphasis on preparation and technical softball has brought her much success. For her to reevaluate her priorities to improve in the areas of loving and connecting with her team was a brave step indeed. She continues:

Chapter 3. Loving Your Players

After receiving word of the issues, I sent out a group message letting the team know practice that day was canceled but to meet at the field. I ask the question to the team as I and I am sure many other coaches have asked their teams before, "How are we doing? How is the team?" And every single time I get the same answer, "We are good." It is like passing someone in the grocery store, "Hey, how are you?" We all ask it, but most importantly we all just want a quick "I am fine" answer. I began to talk to the team and slowly they started to unveil some issues, and the team as a whole, for the first time, confronted together our lack of cohesion. After talking for a couple of hours in the dugout, I asked them, "With us not being connected, will 500 swings get us better? Will 1,000 reps help us?" We all knew the answer. Continuing on in that state I can go ahead and tell you our season. We will be about .500 on the year, maybe win a couple conference awards, and probably make a good run at conference and come home maybe third or fourth place. Oh and we will have completed our monthly community service projects and remain the top sport on campus with most volunteer events. That would be our year. So what do we do? How do we fix it?

Coach Chrietzberg determined that change needed to happen, and she was ready to start the process. She had to put softball skill building on hold so that her team could bond with her and with each other.

My solution was to start an ongoing effort of implementing weekly team time. I told them we would not pick up a ball or swing a bat until they proved to me and my assistant that this team was committed to that task and we were going in the right direction. They had to get together, on their own time (outside of weights, which we continued to do), and text us a picture of them hanging out. Once they did that, we would start back. That was on Monday. We had team bonding weights, we held practices as usual during that week, but never did anything "softball."

Coach Crietzberg ultimately changed the culture of her team and changed herself in the process. She summarizes the metamorphosis that literally happened right before her eyes:

It has been amazing to see the transformation this team has made in just a few short weeks since then. While we still may go .500 on the year, I believe we have found something more than that. Behind the results of whatever this team may do, you are going to find love. You will see that this team had fun together. They made new friends and learned more about themselves. And hopefully through it all they will leave their college experience having found their bridesmaids, which is my first goal whenever I got into coaching. It takes time to invest in each of these beautiful ladies, but it is vital and it is also what gets the best out of them. I told them they must take this time to invest in the health of the team, and in turn, the coaching staff will give up practice time to allow them to spend time together as well. I also do what we call "January meetings" each year. At these we sit down with each and every player individual and just talk. We tell them we will talk about anything except softball. We ask how classes are going, discuss their major, how is their family, boyfriend, etc. It is our time to get closer to them as an individual and learn about them. I am constantly battling with myself on stepping back and taking time to just talk with them each day. To back away from being on task and on time and one more rep but stopping what I am doing and truly caring about how they are and how their day went. I have found I can coach them better, if I can first show them I care. I can get the best out of them and be the hardest on them if I show them love first.

What she did changed her from a good, solid coach into a great one.

Two-time All-American from the University of Oregon Jenna Lilley writes about a very special coach who impacted her life beyond softball. The former Team USA third baseman and current Chicago Bandit tells us lets us about a very special coach, Jimmy Kolaitis:

Casey Chrietzberg, 2017.

> Coach K has made a tremendous impact on my life. It's been almost two years since I've played for him, yet will still talk several times per week. Coach K was a rock for

Chapter 3. Loving Your Players

our team and truly cared about each and every one of his players as people.

When I showed up on campus as a freshman, and quite frankly, for my first two years of college, I was all softball, softball, softball. I had it made up in my (stubborn) mind that I was going to play until I was in my mid to late 30's and coach collegiately. Coach K would always ask me what I wanted to do with my life, and I repeatedly said, "Play and coach softball forever." Coach wouldn't accept that answer. He challenged me to see what else was out there, what my other interests might be. We had this conversation countless times throughout my career. He got me thinking about life after softball, and I am so thankful for him and those conversations we had. He helped me to see the bigger picture in life, and what this was really about. He would always ask about school, how my classes were going, how my family was, and how I was really doing. Coach K took the time to get to know us each as individuals and the type of people we were, and pushed us to be our best in every aspect of our lives whether it was on the field, in school, the relationships we had, etc.

On top of all this, yes, he is also an incredible coach and hitting guru. Coach K flat out knows his stuff, and more importantly, he was a great teacher who was always willing to keep learning himself. He would always be there for us to get in extra work whenever we wanted. Whether you were in the starting nine or the last one off the bench, Coach would be there for you to get better, and you could really feel that in the way he interacted with you. During these extra sessions most of the time they would turn into life talks. Sure, we got in great work, but we also had a great time doing it.

As an athlete, I played with a lot of emotion and passion. During games and practice, Coach K was always there to help calm me down without judgment. He was the presence I needed to relax after a bad at bat. I needed my 30 seconds to destress from an at bat, those times were crucial for me to fully release and move on to the next play. Coach understood that and helped me walk through my at bats and talk to me about what adjustments I needed to make. Anytime I went up to bat, I could still hear him in my ear. We were a team at the plate. We were doing it together. We put so much work in together that it carried over when I stepped into the box, and I could really feel a strong connection with him at the plate.

As the old saying goes (something like this?), you won't remember the wins and the losses but you'll remember the memories you made with your teammates. For me, the same goes with my coaches. I will always remember the memories we made along the way during the great, and not so great, times.

I feel very fortunate to have had a great experience with every one of my coaches during my time at the University of Oregon. I could tell similar stories about Mike White, Chelsea Spencer, Kailee Cuico-Spencer, and Mark Dillon (strength coach) that I've written about Jimmy. This staff was something special. Our staff and players were a family, we shared such a tight knit bond. It wasn't all rainbows, but at the end of the day, we genuinely cared about each other. I would have run through a wall for any of my coaches and teammates.

An Academic All-American utility player cannot say enough about the love of her college coach for her and her team. To be this kind of a coach should be the goal of every one of us:

> A coach I connected with throughout the years has been my college coach. As hard-headed as he may be, he has one of the biggest hearts of anyone I know. He has been around the field for a long time but he could tell you just about every player he has ever had. He has a big presence for sure, but he uses it to make an impact on more people than he could imagine. He is one of the biggest advocates for his girls and will talk someone's ear off to fight for us or even just to chat. A few things I have learned about him are he always has a joke to crack but he can take them too, he definitely can't dance but he does it anyway because he knows it will get a good laugh, and he wants you to do well in every aspect of life even more than he does softball. He knows every

Jenna Lilley, 2018.

Chapter 3. Loving Your Players

little thing about everyone and checks in on you just to stay updated on the littlest things sometimes but is always there when the big stuff comes around too. I think the way he connects with people is very genuine; he is a busy guy but the fact that he keeps up with what you're going through means a lot. I have had two knee injuries, both of which happened on the field during a game, and he carried me off both times. When I was doing rehab with the trainers he'd come in and see where I was at and how I was feeling; most of the time I'd respond, "The same as yesterday," but he'd still come in the next day and ask the same thing. All he had done to connect was to learn about us the same way we learned about him. He wants so much for all of his players. Regardless of what happens on the field, he wants the best for each and every one of us and that makes you feel important.

We have heard about many different types of expressions of love between coach and athlete. If nothing else we see that a specific manner of expression is not demanded by our players, only that we be genuine and purposeful in expressing our love. Feeling loved is important to our softball players. Their performance is tied to our ability to make them feel cared about. It could be argued that this need is a strength and not a weakness. Feeling loved by a coach they respect allows the female athlete to engage with her sport on every level, giving her all, knowing that her coach loves and supports her no matter the outcome of her athletic efforts.

This is another component of coaching female athletes that comes with the territory.

Experiencing love from their coach is not an essential for the male athlete. Knowing that their coach loves them outside of the court or the field is not as important to them. They want a coach who has the formula to win, regardless of the bond between them. They desire that their coach respect them for their athletic abilities and reward them with the opportunities to get on the field. This is the emphasis in sports that males look for. The recognition and respect that comes from being a "starter" trumps feeling loved and cared about as a person. The pregame theatrics of announcing the starters for a contest by name (but not the rest of the players) accentuates this moment of recognition that drives the male athlete. This is what he desires from the coach, his respect and recognition. A relationship of love off the field? Not so much. While male athletes may place less importance on feeling loved by their coach, for the female it is an aspect of coaching success we cannot afford to ignore.

Chapter 4

Leading Your Players

The leadership attributes our players are looking for are not just strength or confidence. These cost us nothing and do not demonstrate our commitment to them. They are looking for a leader who is selfless, someone who puts them first. If our interactions with them are that of an authoritarian boss to an employee, we have failed as a leader. If we want to lead them, we must serve them every chance we get. We should do things we don't have to do for them.

We may feel that we are effective leaders, but only 75 percent of players surveyed answered true to the statement, "I consider my coach to be a good leader."

Players share the attributes they look for in a coach.

An outstanding pitcher speaks of the leadership of a college coach who cared about more than softball. "This coach was a leader on and off the field. Specifically, she pushed for exceptional grades in the classroom and expected her players to maintain a degree of academic excellence. Study hall was mandatory, and as inconsequential of a rule as I believed it was at the time, it helped me as an athlete develop crucial time management skills. Furthermore, those time management skills that I nurtured as a college student have been an integral component in my post collegiate success and have helped me excel in my professional career."

Her coach, her leader went beyond thinking of this person as just an athlete. She was determined to lead her in a path that would ensure her success far beyond her playing days. This player went on to have a successful career as an attorney. No doubt her coach's leadership on the softball field played a part in it.

Another attribute female athletes look for in a leader is someone who protects them and has their back. I witnessed a college softball game where the coach of the winning team was a high-profile personality, highly revered in the softball world. During the game some bad blood had shown itself between the teams to the point where words

Chapter 4. Leading Your Players

were spoken between players. During the post-game "good sportsmanship" line, tensions ran high as some on the winning team actually spit in their hands before touching hands with their opponents. One of the players on the losing team who had been involved in the war of words during the game refused to touch hands with anyone on the winning team. The high-profile, winning coach took offense to this and pulled the opposing player out of line and began to scold her. At this point, instead of sticking up for her player and backing the high-profile coach down, the coach said nothing, too intimidated to get her player's back. Seeing that her coach, her leader was leaving her on her own to deal with the situation, the player told the big-time coach what her coach should have: "Don't talk to me, you're not my coach." That episode set the respect level that player had for her coach from then on: virtually none. We can be sure that the rest of the team took notice of their coach's lack of leadership. Perhaps that player needed correction in the situation, but it should have been made by her coach. The coach made a costly mistake that day, one that may have been unfixable.

The necessity for us as coaches to have our players' backs can take many forms or modes. From the obvious things like arguing a questionable call that went against our player to standing with them when a professor is not accommodating her on a mid-term when the team is scheduled for an extended road trip.

I had to stand up for my players in a most unexpected way when we were eating at a restaurant late one Sunday night on the way back from Indiana. The team was seated at one large table in an otherwise empty room while I was sitting in a booth nearby with the bus driver. An inebriated man suddenly appeared from the bar area and made his way to the team's table, a large walking stick in one hand and a drink in the other. Around his neck was a baseball size stone with a string necklace running through it. I watched as he stood behind the chairs of two of our players and placed his drink on the table. With slurred speech and inappropriately close to our players, he began to talk about the rock around his neck and to ask questions to the group at large. I could see that this was making the players uncomfortable and seeing no employees in the room, I told the man to take his rock and leave the room ... now. Perhaps a wiser plan of action would have been to find the manager and have him peacefully removed, but honestly, I lose my patience quickly with characters like this man, and I wasn't going to allow him near our players.

Thankfully, the man took one look me and the bus driver (a burly, rough-looking character), apologized profusely to me and left the room.

Coaching Women's Softball

Independently of whether I handled the conflict properly, my relationship with the team in that first year took a giant step forward. They knew I had their backs no matter what the situation.

Our players are looking for someone who is strong and grounded to guide them as players and as people. The high school and college years are times of great change and personal growth. There are decisions to be made, temptations to be avoided, and pressure to manage. During this daunting yet wonderful time our athletes are looking to us to be steady, immovable, and emotionally strong.

I learned early on in my career as a federal agent that success in gaining the cooperation of criminals depended on my relationship with them. The criminal sitting in an interrogation room being questioned about his crimes is in a bad place. What was the best way to get a confession from a hardened criminal or to convince him to turn on his associates? Though there are many techniques or tricks, what the criminal is looking for is someone strong to lead them through this situation with the least amount of damage. What criminals are drawn to is a steady and trustworthy leader. I found that if I presented myself as trustworthy as well as stable and strong, they would believe that I would keep my promises and lead them out of the mess they created. Even hardened criminals are looking for a strong leader. So are our players.

Our players are also looking for predictability in their coach, a leader who doesn't require ego driven confrontations and displays of power. An All-Conference pitcher explains: "Coaches I've had that have been great leaders have had no ego. They do not pretend to be the smartest person in the room and understand they have something to learn from everyone." This perceptive player has put her finger on a major barrier to effective leadership, one that affects many otherwise great coaches. It is our ego that can plunge us into situations we should have avoided and arguments that were simply unnecessary. I have seen coaches with enormous egos talk down to anyone they feel superior to, including their players and assistant coaches. Thinking they are larger than life and respected by all, in reality they are simply rude and arrogant. If we intend to lead our players, we need to keep our egos in check.

Longtime William Peace University Head Coach and former member of the legendary "King and His Court" Charlie Dobbins concurs: "You don't know everything. This goal, if it is to be attained, must be a collaboration of everyone involved in the process. Explain to the team your ideas, but leave room for feedback from the other parts of the team,

Chapter 4. Leading Your Players

namely your assistant coaches, players and other individuals that make up the program."

Where many coaches lose in their efforts to be a respected leader of their team is their behavior during competition, in the "heat of battle." Instead of a calm, collected battlefield general, many coaches act like nervous, frightened, newly enlisted privates, losing their composure and blowing their cool. These uptight coaches are unapproachable before and during games as they emit vibes that keep everyone back. While our team wants to stay loose during games, we can be irritable, preoccupied, and angry. Adopting the mood we set, our team takes on our nervous demeanor, and all confidence drains out. Entering a game uptight and fretting about what could go wrong is a certain recipe for defeat.

The same former pitcher elaborates: "Another quality I've seen in coaches that have been great leaders is the ability to maintain composure, positive and negative. This facilitates a no stress environment for the team. To know that your coach is not stressed about the score, the other team, etc. makes a huge difference in the attitude of the team and the way they play."

Charlie Dobbins, 2012.

Coaching Women's Softball

An All-Region outfielder with a career batting average over .400 talks about the effect a coach who loses his composure has on her: "I found it easy to lose respect for coaches when they ignorantly argued with umpires. Now, there is a time and place to argue calls and a demeanor to hold when you do so. Momentous points of the game, having your player's back, and legitimate rule calls should have conversation. Yes, there are times that even coaches get caught in the heat of the moment, but as a coach and the head of your team, you should always have the ability to display your point without seeming ignorant."

Coach Charlie Dobbins emphasizes the need for coaches to bring a steadying influence to the team: "Your job is not to be too high or too low. In the heat of the moment it can be easy to lose sight of your vision by leading with the wrong tone."

Coach Dobbins' picture of a steady, controlled coach making decisions with a clear mind stands in contrast with what we have seen way too often: coaches who disrespectfully and often unnecessarily argue with umpires and coaches who chastise players during games for unintentional mistakes. These coaches are like a pot of 211-degree water, just waiting for their pitcher to give up a walk or an outfielder to misjudge a fly ball. These are the types who become more agitated, more nervous, and more angry with every run that the other team scores. This Jekyll and Hyde coach turns from Mr. Confident at the game's first pitch to a red-faced, cursing machine in the third inning down 4–0.

Our players don't want the volatile coach I described as their leader. They don't trust him. They have their hands full managing their own emotions during games and look for someone steady to plug in to. They want to know that no matter what transpires on the field that day, coach will handle it, coach will protect them. To be the leader our players seek, we must be passionate and competitive, but we must also be controlled and confident.

This internal strength, this high level of confidence coupled without the need to have her ego massaged, is what an All-Region outfielder seeks in her coach: "A leader to me is someone who does the job without searching for the praise. Someone who is always there for players, but lets them shine in their successes. A leader is someone who holds the strongest in controversy and keeps calm in the crazy. The confidence a true leader displays is what makes me follow them."

The inability of a coach to manage his emotions is something that can undo everything positive that has been done to establish himself as a leader. I coached for many years on a travel team under a great

Chapter 4. Leading Your Players

coach who could not control his pre-game emotions. A former professional baseball player, his competitive juices would run so strong during warm-ups that his outbursts of anger would cast a negative cloud over the team. These highly motivated, teenaged athletes, all destined to secure college softball scholarships, would dread his pre-game antics. Here was an extremely knowledgeable coach, a great connector who loved his players but unable to control his emotions. At the moment when a coach should display calmness and confidence, he would become extremely agitated, yelling at his players due to his own case of nerves.

A leader is secure, willing to listen and willing to put the team's interests above the wants of any individual player. A Division I pitcher learned this lesson in a single conversation. Going into her senior year of high school, a new coach was hired. As a senior leader of the team she was initially distrusting of her and skeptical of the changes she was making. She tells the story of a memorable meeting they had:

> As the season continued I began sitting closer to Coach to listen to how she would talk about what was happening in the game with our same dependable assistant coach that everyone loved. I remember at one point she stopped allowing me to play first when I wasn't pitching, which I didn't like. I knew I was a good first baseman, as I was going to get to play there in college as well as pitch. I asked to talk to her about it. I had written my thoughts down. When I got to our meeting coach took my notes from me and read them and just smiled at me. She said, "Okay, talk." I told her what I thought. She said, "Ok, my turn." She explained to me she didn't disagree I was a good first baseman and would do well in college, but it was the beginning of the season. We were playing games that didn't count for area, regionals or the state tournament. She told me she knew once we got to state this year, she knew I would be on the mound during the majority of the tournament. She asked me how I was planning to pitch and play first at the same exact time. She explained she had to develop other players there before the games that mattered started, and asked how was it fair to my teammates if she just threw them into a position during the most important tournament if she had not given them prior game experience. She told me I was thinking of now, and she was planning for the future and what I wanted, the state championship. She also told me I have college to look to, but she has to think of the high school program's future and as a whole. Then she looked at me and said, "I trust you on the field, why don't you trust me and just see what happens? This is your senior year. Have you ever been to the state championship before?" The answer was no. She then said, "Then what do you have to

lose? I promise you we are going to the state tournament this year." I left that meeting with a total new outlook. No coach had ever talked like that to me before. She had allowed me to talk first and listened. She earned my trust completely in just that one meeting.

Her coach's willingness to converse, listen to concerns, provide a limited explanation, and finally to ask for the player's trust resulted in complete loyalty from that pitcher. As a senior leader that player certainly was an influence on the team to respect their coach.

Birmingham Southern Coach Kimball Cassady recalls the inspiration she drew as a player from Coach Les Studeman: "The best coach I ever had and learned so much from is Les Stuedeman. Something about her and her coaching philosophy made me want to be the best I could be. She pushed me to limits and although she stayed on me like white on rice, I knew she believed in me and wanted me to be the best version of myself. I remember her telling me, 'When I quit speaking to you, that's when you need to start worrying.' Well, apparently, I had nothing to worry about!"

This ability to inspire, to motivate and to instill confidence is cited by a standout third baseman:

> A great leader is one who inspires and challenges a group and every individual in it to strive to be among the elite. A great leader is one who makes you feel it, to make you want to do great things on the field. A great leader isn't someone who just says all the right things and checks all the right boxes, but someone you feel inspired by, one who feels inspired themselves. A great leader is one who is excited to come to work each and every day and is willing to do all the work necessary to achieve an elite level.

An infielder describes the ability of her coach to adapt his coaching style to each individual player: "Coach is truly a chameleon and that's what makes him a great coach. He knows that not every player is the same, so he doesn't treat them that way. He constantly picked up players when they were down and never lost hope in a player."

Our task as leaders is to fan the flames of competitiveness that exist within our players. Softball, at any level other than a beginning recreational program, is not for the passive. Encouraging competitiveness is doable and is something that we can embrace. We take the desire to compete that exists in our players and seek to increase it exponentially. As coaches and leaders, we need to model the competitiveness we want to see in our players. We share our need to win with positive words.

Chapter 4. Leading Your Players

Negative statements that signal a lack of confidence cannot come out of our mouths. Ever. Pre-game nerves can cause us to send all the wrong messages with our body language alone. By our words and demeanor, we must communicate that we welcome all challenges with no backing up. Our players must know that their coach is not intimidated by any opponent and that we enter every contest with the expectation of winning. We are the ones who provide the confidence to meld with their competitiveness. As they see a confident leader who is hyper-competitive as well, they will draw strength for the battle.

Competitiveness in a coach is a quality that is essential if we are to maximize our players' performances. They are watching to see just how deep our own need to win goes, and this is revealed best in our behavior and our words when we lose. When we have a meltdown after a loss, we can compound the effect of losing the game by losing our composure. Instead of being constructive and unshakable, we can get caught up in a lengthy tirade where we signal that our confidence in the team and in ourselves was thin and easily shattered. We can deliver hard words if appropriate, but we do so without appearing as someone whose confidence has been stolen by the loss of a game. Be real and be corrective, but at the same time be constructive and optimistic, letting your team know that your competitive fires are still burning. They should know that it takes more than a loss to knock their coach out. They should walk away from a loss with more than just adjustments to be made. They should leave knowing that their coach still believes, that their coach's confidence and competitiveness are both unshakable.

This infusion of confidence is something each of us does differently, but do it we must. For me, it what was instilled into me as a young police officer in Miami. It was drilled into me that if I wanted to go home every night, I had to win in every situation. Whether it was overcoming an armed suspect or fighting with people who attacked me, I was going to win. As an ATF Special Agent, many times I was in a dangerous place, making an arrest of a violent felon, executing a search warrant, or working in an undercover operation. In all cases, I win, you lose, and I go home to my family. This is the attitude I carry deep within me even years removed from the job. This is what I quietly portray with the expectation that it will elevate the level of confidence my players have on game day. Our attitude of confidence is what bolsters our players. Words are great, but being that competitive person yourself is what motivates and builds the competitiveness we seek in our players.

A former All-Conference pitcher speaks of the ability to motivate each individual on the team as a critical characteristic of leadership: "Coaches who are great leaders are able to motivate everyone on the team individually. That kind of coach listens and knows how to get each individual to perform to their maximum potential. A great leader guides the team on how to play and win, but lets the players express and play to their individual strengths. Not all players are motivated in the same way and or need it to the same extent."

The travel ball coach I coached with (mentioned above) was the best I've seen at this. He was capable of motivating every player on the team, each in a slightly different way. For the hyper-competitive player who was entirely self motivated, he would offer a calming presence. He would challenge the slightly lazy, speak confidence to the unsure, and bring down the arrogant a notch when necessary. He knew what each of his players lacked, and he figured out a way to give that to them.

Learning enough about each player, getting to know her well enough to be able to motivate her, is not a job for the lazy among us. It will take observation, conversation, and a whole lot of listening. While we have been conditioned to think success on the field is the sum of technique and practice (X's and O's), it comes down to being able to lead each player.

Mike Davenport, in his twentieth season as Head Coach at the University of North Georgia, understands the importance of leading his best players. He points out that it is often the better players who receive less of our attention and leadership. As an eight-time conference Coach of the Year and 2015 Division II National Champion, he speaks from a place of success:

> I learned years ago, and am still guilty as a coach doing this or "not" doing this. In coaching we spend a lot of time addressing the failures or the weaknesses of each team and/or player. If we have a player that is struggling on or off the field and we feel that they may be affecting the team, we often spend a lot of time and energy hoping to improve the situation in hopes to improve the overall team.
>
> One player that often gets neglected in this process is your "best" player. When I was a young student-assistant baseball coach at a junior college, our best player struggled on the field for about a month. And like we often do as coaches, we know/feel that they will get it figured out and get back to their level of play, so we stay away from that athlete. This particular player and I became pretty good friends still today, and I will never forget him asking us as coaches a year or so after his career had ended as to why we didn't challenge him like we did the other players. He stated that all he needed at the time was a push to get back to the level he knew he could play at.

Chapter 4. Leading Your Players

So as a learning opportunity early in my coaching profession, I have worked to make it a point to focus on the needs of your most talented players to assist them as much if not more than all of your other players.

Coach Anson Dorrance speaks with the authority of winning over 800 NCAA Division I women's soccer games and 22 NCAA Championships:

> Perhaps the best way to view coaching women is to explore how different it can be from coaching men. In fact, our program at UNC is largely defined by the social (and yes, athletic) differences between men and women. And while we as coaches never want to cease learning about our sport, ultimately coaching development ceases to be about finding newer ways to organize practice. In other words you soon stop collecting drills. Your coaching development shifts to observing how to support and motivate your players and how to lead them to perform at higher and higher levels.[*]

Coach Dorrance makes the point that real coaching is not about having the best practice drills. More important for our success as

Mike Davenport, 2019.

[*]Dorrance, "Coaching Women."

coaches of female athletes is our ability to support and motivate them. The support they require goes far beyond a pat on the back that might suffice for the typical male athlete. They must feel that we have faith in them and will back them even if they struggle. The support they seek is built upon us making the effort to know them as people. They want to know that we see them for who they are, and that we like what we see. Coach Danson uses the word "observe" as the key to knowing how to support and motivate our players. Observation takes time, as does the analysis of our observations. Considering what we observe in every player, we are able to formulate a game plan to be what we need to be for them and for the success of the program.

We must arm ourselves with the knowledge of how to individually motivate, how to make our players want to follow our leadership and to value our approval. If we commit to improving in this area, it will take time and effort, but coaches (and their staff) who get this will be amazed at the results. The energy we spent raging, fretting, snapping, and shaming players needs to be diverted to the task of motivating individuals to excel and to win softball games.

A former All-Conference pitcher takes it a step further as she speaks of the ability to motivate each individual on the team as a critical characteristic of leadership: "Coaches who are great leaders are able to motivate everyone on the team individually. That kind of coach listens and knows how to get each individual to perform to their maximum potential. A great leader guides the team on how to play and win, but lets the players express and play to their individual strengths. Not all players are motivated in the same way and or need it to the same extent."

A standout infielder explains how a great leader knows about the many faces of failure. A coach who leads well knows when a player's failure to perform is related to something that is simply part of the game. Mental errors, a poor attitude, or lack of effort is another matter entirely and calls for a different coaching response.

> I had a coach who never punished us for failing—for the things that were just part of the game—strikeouts, bad hops, errors. These were physical errors, not mental ones. We were only chewed out when we made a mental mistake—not communicating, wearing the wrong uniform, not encouraging out teammates. Because of this we played with our hearts out because we knew that we would not be punished for things outside of our control. We were in charge of our attitudes and our effort and we knew that is all the coach expected from us. With

Chapter 4. Leading Your Players

this coach, we had many undefeated seasons, overall great team batting averages, and great fielding percentages.

On the other hand, I had a coach who would punish us for practically everything. If we weren't perfect, we would stay at practice until we were. If we made one error, that would be what coach would harp on after the game was over. Bad hops were always our fault and we just "needed to be better." Needless to say, we had a terrible season, we were burnt out, down on ourselves, and struggled to keep positive attitudes.

What happens is that the coaches who punish young women for not being perfect are setting a precedent in their adult lives. How we praise and punish young women makes a difference about how they see themselves in their adult lives. Young women who are taught to control what they can control and expect failure in order to be great become leaders and confident. Those who were punished countlessly for failing and things outside of their control go through life walking on eggshells, afraid to make a mistake. You should never play ball on eggshells just like you should never go through life on eggshells.

An All-Conference pitcher cites hard work as a leadership trait that resonates with her. A true coach should lead with excitement and should be eager to engage with her players. The willingness of this great coach to give of herself, to teach, explain, drill and simply stay late is why players respected and followed her. "One of my coaches in college who I would consider a great leader was the first person at practice and the last to leave. If you wanted extra help in the hitting cages or taking grounders, she would stay late. She always allowed me to learn new things at my own pace and understood that everyone learns in different ways so she would find new ways of explaining and teaching concepts. This made everyone want to be the best for her."

An All-Region outfielder also connects the individual attention she received from her coach with great leadership: "One coach that most impacted me was the one who took time to get me out of a slump. Instead of just letting me go through the motions and stay in a pity party, she took time to break down my swing to the barest and most raw level and build me back up. With this, my confidence rose, my softball sense rose, and my will to win returned."

Our players are looking to us to set the tone both in attitude and in work product. We cannot expect these virtues from our team if we don't mirror them. Our success as a leader begins with how we choose to approach our sport. As William Peace Coach Charlie Dobbins writes:

"Show enthusiasm for your sport as an individual and as the leader of your team. People will follow you as this is infectious. It will lead to increased dedication and commitment."

Snead State Coach Tracy Grindrod writes of the role of passion and enthusiasm in leadership. He speaks as the winner of two JUCO National Championships: "When you sense the energy level is down on the team, it is up to you to get it cranked up again. This sport is greatly impacted by momentum. When you bring passion and enthusiasm to the team, you can keep momentum on your side."

Another characteristic essential to leading our players is authenticity. We should be aware that our players are great at detecting fakery. If we really don't care for our athletes as people, if we are not leading out of a framework of sincerity and transparency, don't think for a second that our entire team doesn't read us loud and clear.

An All-Region outfielder speaks of the impact of a transparent coach: "One coach I had who was particularly transparent was one that most of the team went to for advice. This coach shared parts of themselves with players where appropriate and knew how to get players to relax, laugh, and enjoy the game. Being transparent and authentic is good but being fake and whining to players is a turn off."

An All-Conference and NFCA National Pitcher of the Week tells of how an authentic coach she had as a 9-year-old set her in motion for a successful collegiate career:

> I had a coach in 10 and under that had a solid impact on the remainder of my career. He was as authentic and transparent as they come. I would not have made it as far as I did without the beginning that he gave me. He not only believed in me but was very honest with me as well. He celebrated the great moments, danced in the dugouts, shouted with joy even. If I was struggling he held me accountable and let me know. I was only 9 but he knew how to motivate me and keep me throwing. He was tough on me, there were times where I did not like him at all, but I knew that he had my best interest at heart. He always made sure that I knew my potential but never blew my head up. He taught me how to handle hard moments, and celebrate the great ones.

A huge component of authenticity is truthfulness. Lying to a player is the deathblow to your success as a coach. Never promise anything that you absolutely don't intend to deliver. If you make false promises, or don't follow through on a verbal commitment to one player, it will have the same effect as if you lied to all.

Chapter 4. Leading Your Players

An All-Region outfielder and former National Player of the Week appreciates the transparency and authenticity her coach operates under:

> When I hear the words authentic and transparent when thinking about the coaches I've played for, my college head coach is the first person that comes to mind. I respected the fact that she would always be up front with her players about the guidelines she put in place and about what she expected out of us. I wouldn't say that playing for her was always easy, but something that she would instill in us is that "winning is fun, but winning is hard work and hard work isn't always fun." She was never the type of coach to sugar coat anything; she is the "what you see is what you get" kind of coach, which is what I liked about her. Even though she pushes her players mentally, physically, and spiritually, we always knew exactly what to expect from her and in the end she prepared us for far more than the game of softball.

Trevecca Nazarene Coach Ben Tyree boils it down to doing what you say: "When you tell your players you will do this or that, one thing you have to do just like you do with your own children: do what you said you would do."

Authenticity is the one topic upon which every survey respondent agreed. When presented with the statement, "It is very important to the success of the team that the coach be real and authentic," 100 percent marked "True." It's that important. In other words, if you can be nothing else, at least be authentic. You cannot begin to lead without authenticity.

Although authenticity was highly valued by players, 25 percent answered "True" to the statement, "My coach lied to me or a teammate." So, what the players want is a coach who is real, authentic, and truthful, yet a fourth of the respondents considered their coach to be a liar. Whether or not we lied, the perception is there. A non-authentic person is a fake whose true motives remain hidden. The lack of trust created when a coach is not real and authentic can bring a program down. Our players aren't asking for perfection from us, just that we be real, that we be the person we claim to be. Our team will not respond to us if we are any less than that.

An All-Conference catcher shares the impact of having a coach go back on her word: "After being selected as Captains, we privately met with our coach on behalf of our team. We asked our coach to consider removing a toxic player from the lineup until they could get their attitude in-check. Our coach agreed and committed to this. The very next time we were down a few runs, our coach went back on her word out of fear of losing that game. What this coach did not realize is that while we didn't lose the game, she did lose her Captains' respect."

Another former player, a power-hitting infielder speaks of another form of untruthfulness, when a coach promises to enforce certain standards but then alters those standards mid-stream:

> A coach has lost my respect when there are inconsistencies between what they preach to the team and what they do. A previous coach I had set standards and put disciplines into place towards beginning of year, and then failed to hold people accountable to those standards through the end of the season. The thing about discipline is that it only can enhance a team if everyone is held accountable, regardless of the circumstances. When a coach doesn't stay true to their word it makes the team think that she isn't committed to do whatever it takes to be successful. It makes it challenging once a player loses trust for a coach. Great teams are a unit and require a great coach, great players, and great culture between the two. When a coach, the leader of the team, loses the trust of the players, the unit is incomplete and not performing at maximum level.

As coaches we cannot afford to look for excuses for why certain players are not responding to our leadership and to conclude that it is

Courtnay Foster, 2018.

Chapter 4. Leading Your Players

the player's fault, not ours. The labeling of a generation as being "entitled," for instance, does not take us off the hook; it is incumbent upon us to find a way to lead.

Former All-American at Northwestern University and current University of Alabama Birmingham (UAB) Associate Head Coach Courtnay Foster explains her approach to the "entitled" generation: "Throughout leadership and coaching circles I often hear phrases such as 'millennials are an entitled generation' or 'millennials are not tough.' As my thoughts on these observations tend to lean towards agreement, I also believe that it is more important to consider the reason for their condition and not simply that they are what they are. I also strongly believe that all humans are at least in part a product of the way they have been conditioned by their environment and that one's habituation is not a constant, but rather an ever-changing learned response."

Volumes have been written about how to manage "Millennials" or more relevant today "Generation Z" in the workplace and on the athletic field. We as coaches need to become familiar with the general characteristics of these generational groups. Understanding their attitudes towards others, competing, and work ethic will help us formulate our own game plan to reach and motivate them in a way that we and our players can both live with.

We may see leading as issuing commands, setting schedules and making line-up cards, but our players are looking for a different kind of leader. To the female athlete, the role of "coach" does not necessarily make us the leader. Unless we make a concerted effort to be the leader of our team, the players will crown their own.

Even if we don't believe that one our players will replace us as the de facto leader, this happens quite often. Though we may believe we are steering the ship, we may not be. Surprisingly, 40 percent of the surveyed softball players marked "True" to the statement, "One of my teammates is the true leader of my team instead of the coach."

If we won't lead in a way that inspires our players, we may be unable to hang on to that position. Unfortunately, the player selected to be the informal yet de facto leader is often the very player we do not want having an influence on our team. It is often the toxic, narcissistic players that actually do have leadership qualities that draw followers, but these are leading our team away from us. While conventional wisdom tells us that we need strong leaders on the team, just who gets to become that leader is something we often leave to chance. Allowing the team to choose their own captains is an exercise that can go terribly wrong.

Players taking on a limited leadership role on our team is a good thing, provided we as coaches are in control of who those leaders are.

More importantly, we cannot afford to leave an empty chair where we as coaches should be sitting. If we leave a void, if we mail in our leadership duties, it is likely that a disruptive influence is waiting to fill that space. A player with some charisma, someone who is naturally influential, can take the leadership reins, and you may have a difficult time getting them back.

An All-Region pitcher describes this very situation, when the coach is not considered the leader of the program: "I never really looked at my coach as a leader. To be honest, I always felt like the players were more so the leaders and with my experience responsibility was given out to the players to try and get the other players in line and on the same correct page."

In summary, it is our obligation and privilege to lead a team of female athletes. It is our challenge and our duty to understand and lead each of them. They have told us what they want from us, which is simply everything. They have placed their order, and it is a tall one. They want an emotionally secure disciplinarian who has their back at all times. They want us to be calm and confident yet hyper-competitive. They seek a highly knowledgeable yet humble teacher of the game. Someone who is an inspirational motivator who quietly works harder than anyone on the team. Most of all an authentic, transparent leader.

Chapter 5

Praise and Appreciation

It is not enough to appreciate effort and attitude; we as coaches must open our mouths and acknowledge them. Female athletes need to hear it. Hear that their effort has not gone unnoticed. Hear that their great attitude is appreciated. To be heard, we must speak—often, frequently, every time it is warranted. Recognize, recognize, recognize. Notice the extra effort at practice and praise it. Learn of their off the field accomplishments, in the classroom or doing charitable activities, for example. Give praise and recognition for these life accomplishments, even if they are unrelated to her sport.

Trevecca Nazarene University Coach Ben Tyree, whose Trojans led all of NCAA Division II in batting average in 2019, also places a high priority on praising his players: "Players never get enough praise and I always give my players a chance to tell the team what is going well and what is not going so well without embarrassing them in front of their teammates. But at the end of the day, a pat on the back or telling someone how well they are doing will go a long way to have a successful season. You always need to praise them for doing things you expect them to do."

South Carolina Head Coach Beverly Smith describes the systematic process her team employs to communicate praise and positive statements called "Proud Ofs." This exercise takes very little time but yields large results as players are recognized and affirmed.

> In a world where it is so easy to criticize, hold on to the negative, and watch the errors/strikeouts on loop on social media, I think it is important as coaches to consistently allow time for positive feedback. At South Carolina, at the end of a three (3) game series or tournament weekend, my team will do "Proud Ofs." The execution is simple; guidelines are below.
>
> 1. Team stands in a circle. Coach reminds players the standard for Proud Ofs
>   a. Each player will choose a teammate to shout out and then will give a personal "Proud Of."

    b. Comments must be specific and cannot be repeated.
    c. Encourage eye contact when giving and receiving feedback.
    d. Speak with confidence, avoid using words Like and Um.
2. The First player states, "I am proud of *teammate* for *specific behavior*"
3. Coach may need to help navigate the conversation if the player is being too vague. What specifically about Susie's performance are you referring to?
4. Once Susie is recognized for her double play—the double play can't be used again.
5. This allows players to reflect and notice the little things. For example, the athlete who picked the change might get a shout-out. The player who picked someone up after a bad at bat, or the pinch runner who scored for the DP.

Coach Note: Listening in the circle, I became aware of things that I did not know happened in the dugout or on the field during the weekend. I would also submit that praise from your peers recognized in front of the team goes a long way. Watch the body language of the person receiving the compliment. Their face opens and body perks up. You will also be aware of what players don't receive any Proud Ofs. The team will not recognize the athletes who are selfish, underperforming or undermining the team. This makes for good mental notes for the coaching staff.

6. After player 1 recognizes their teammate of choice, they need to say what behavior they are proud of themselves for. THIS IS WILDLY MORE DIFFICULT FOR FEMALE ATHLETES and will require some continued coaching. Watch for negative self talk, i.e., So glad I got on base because I struck out both at bats before. Examples:
    a. I am proud of my at bats today because I laid off the rise ball that coach & I discussed.
    b. I was proud of my pre-pitch routine today—I stayed focused on it.
    c. I did not give up a walk today.
    d. I was proud I took an extra base with the ball in the dirt.
    e. I thought I was helpful to the hitters charting the pitcher in the dugout.

Once you have done this and set the expectations, this exercise can be done in 5–8 minutes. I have always lived by the quote, "Reward the behaviors you want to see repeated." There will be a time and a place to review the challenges of the weekend. Proud Ofs gives the platform

Chapter 5. Praise and Appreciation

to recognize the various things you want to repeat as a coach. It is personal, meaningful and positive.

Rather than follow convention and use the post series or tournament wrap up as a stage for proclaiming mistakes, deficiencies, and shortcomings, Coach Smith choses to delay the corrective phase to another time. Instead, she has her team take the post-game energy in a positive direction, with players praising players for legitimate accomplishments and attitudes.

In adopting Proud Ofs as a part of the softball experience at South Carolina, Coach Smith is teaching valuable life lessons that will impact lives far beyond softball. She is teaching her players the value of expressed praise and appreciation, of how to affirm and encourage others. She is also teaching them to how to accept recognition and affirmation.

USA Softball Hall of Famer and current Oregon State Head Coach Laura Berg explains how she makes praise a priority in her program: "It is extremely important to praise your athletes. Not just for hard work & great plays but also for their school work/grades. The way I like to go about praise and appreciation is the Oreo cookie effect. I'll give them praise for something they did. Then I'll give them a criticism and then finish with another praise. We play a sport of failure and these players will fail 70% of the time; they need to be praised by their coaching staff so they don't get down on themselves and over-analyze their failures."

The power of praise was proven in one young 8th grade pitcher who came to me for pitching lessons. She had been an above-average, but not outstanding, pitcher in travel ball and in middle school. After meeting her and her father, I asked her to pitch as I watched without comment. I saw a lot of work that needed to be done, but I also saw talent that

Beverly Smith, 2010.

Coaching Women's Softball

was buried in her. After watching her throw for 30 minutes without giving any feedback, I simply said, "You could be a great pitcher." Her eyes lit up, and she instantly became one of my hardest working students. She progressed nicely through her high school years, and I was lucky enough to be able to have her commit to playing for me in college. Because of her work ethic and natural talent, she went on to be the conference "Pitcher of the Year" as a freshman and was All-Conference every year. She will tell you that her road to success began that evening when I gave her praise, when I expressed confidence in her. The relationship between us that began with a word of praise developed into a strong, very close friendship that still exists today.

The expressions of praise and appreciation by a coach are powerful motivators. Eighty-three percent of those surveyed responded "True" to the statement: "I perform best when my coach expresses praise and appreciation."

Whether players are receiving the amount of praise and appreciation they want is another matter. Only 60 percent of respondents answered "True" to the statement: "My coach gives me the amount of praise and appreciation that I desire."

So, we know that players value praise and appreciation and play harder when they receive it. Yet, though it costs us nothing as coaches to give them what they want in this area, forty percent of the time we aren't getting the job done. We have to ask ourselves why many of us are hesitant to praise our players. Perhaps we were raised without it and are not comfortable praising others or expressing appreciation for their efforts. Maybe we as individuals think we don't need it, so we have trouble understanding why others seek it. No matter how hard-core we may be as people, the truth is that everyone does better when they are appreciated. It is our responsibility to get past whatever reservations we have about praising our players. It is a piece of the coaching puzzle we can't afford to leave out.

A former PAC 12 All-American and current NPF player's story demonstrates just how much our players long for praise and affirmation from us as coaches. In spite of this need, sometimes it is not forthcoming. She heard it from her coach two years after their coach/player relationship was over, but it was extremely significant and memorable for her nonetheless: "My head coach was a man of few words and those words were far from praise, more often than not. The biggest sentiment of appreciation that I ever felt from my coach was two years after my senior season. I had been watching old games and sent him a text about how much I loved playing for him. He replied telling me how much he

Chapter 5. Praise and Appreciation

loved coaching me. It was the highest form of praise I'd ever received from him and I cherish that interaction."

A standout infielder focuses on the impact a word of appreciation can have: "Players aren't complicated; we thrive on succeeding. When you a play a sport such as softball, you fail seven out of ten times, and you are constantly working to always be better. We need to know we are doing well. So when a coach takes the moment to say, 'Hey, you did a phenomenal job today at the plate' or 'Thank you for taking 5 minutes to break down to the new infielders how we manage bunts,' it will mean more than hitting a home run."

Like any human being in any endeavor, players simply want for us as coaches to recognize their effort. As she so aptly puts it, "Players aren't complicated" when it comes to wanting and needing verbal appreciation. It is interesting that she identifies expressions of appreciation as a "need." She doesn't see it as optional for us as coaches. Our players need it and will struggle to operate at 100 percent capacity without it.

A former Big Ten Player of the Year speaks of how she was affected by timely words of praise and appreciation from her coach. Her coach's expression of unconditional acceptance helped her find the confidence she needed to meet the challenges of impending post season play:

> The situation that comes to mind is when we were almost heading into postseason play. I was just talking with one of our coaches who had been amazing pitcher and hitter in college and in the pro league. We were having a more open/deep conversation. I had brought up that pressure was feeling heightened, expectations seemed heightened, and I didn't want to let the coaches down, my family, etc. My coach just looked at me, put her hand on my shoulder, and said there was nothing I could do that would make her not proud of me. That messed up my world for a bit. It meant the world to me and hit me on a heart level. Knowing her love and support and investment in me was unconditional. She had been in my shoes before and she knew just how to offer me the support and praise that I needed to re-find my confidence.

A former Team USA catcher astutely points out that coaches can tend to offer the least amount of praise and appreciation in the years when the players need it most, such as while a collegiate athlete. Her comments underscore the absolute necessity of praise when warranted. She obviously cherishes those times when she was acknowledged and appreciated as a player:

Coaching Women's Softball

Throughout my career, the amount of praise and appreciation I received from coaches decreased. I'm not sure if this phenomenon is healthy for our athletes in this sport. It seems logical to me that an athlete should be given more praise and appreciation during a time in their career when they are working the hardest, spending the most time, and performing the best instead of being expected to perform like a machine, only hearing from a coach when something isn't done to their satisfaction.

Positive reinforcement is powerful. Make players feel good and encourage them to recreate those performances through praise and appreciation. When a coach spoke highly of me, I felt it was my duty as a player to maintain that status. It motivated me to exceed expectations.

I'll share a couple examples I can remember feeling the most praised and appreciated by my coach. I loved when coach would mention my name in a post-game talk, not because of the monster home run I hit in the 5th, but the way I pitch called, managed the pitcher, or led the team. It made me feel like all the little things I was doing to help my team didn't go unnoticed. I didn't want praise from the media; I wanted it from the people I cared about around me.

I also felt super proud when coach would share some of my nuances, techniques, or style of play with younger players in the organization or other teams as if I were example for others. Whether they were watching or not, I felt the responsibility to be that example.

We may resent the fact that our players require our praise, blaming it on them being a part of Generation Z, or the way their parents constantly fed this need. That line of thinking may contain some truth. In some cases, "helicopter parents" have spent every moment praising our players growing up, sometimes when no praise was earned or warranted. These players may have unreasonable expectations as to the type of actions that warrant praise. The fact remains, however, that this is a real "thing" to them, and we would be wise to make the necessary adjustment in our coaching style.

William Peace Head Coach Charlie Dobbins takes it a step further by memorializing special effort. He counts this practice as an essential component to having a winning program: "Collect stories of team members who go the extra mile for the team. These examples honor those who do exceptional work advancing your goals and illustrate your team's vision. They are also tangible reminders of why your team and its values are different from your competition."

Giving praise and expressing appreciation when it is warranted is a painless way for us to upgrade our performance as coaches. The praise

Chapter 5. Praise and Appreciation

they crave is not unearned drivel we pour upon them. They want to earn our praise with real effort and accomplishments, and when they earn it, they want to be recognized. Recognize effort. Recognize attitude. Praise them when warranted. It will work miracles.

We may think that having a system of recognition and rewards is childish, but this is a need that good organizations and managers all recognize. When I worked at the Federal Bureau of Alcohol, Tobacco, Firearms and Explosives, there were systems in place to reward special effort and achievement—systems to ensure that grown hardened men and women were "praised" for their good work. You would think that of all people, law enforcement types wouldn't thrive on praise and appreciation, but they did. The better managers went one step further by personally praising and appreciating the special agents that deserved it.

I still remember my first case as a special agent with the Bureau of Alcohol, Tobacco, Firearms and Explosives. As a young, eager agent, I had identified a violent criminal who was dealing machine guns on the streets of New Orleans and opened up an investigation into his illegal activities. I found a way to meet him while I was in an undercover capacity, gained his confidence, and eventually purchased a number of machine guns from him. After this man's arrest and conviction in federal court, I received a letter of commendation from the Special Agent in Charge for my work on this case. It took him all of ten minutes to compose this letter (who knows, maybe his assistant actually wrote the letter), but the words of that letter remain with me some 37 years later. I was a thirty-year-old former Miami Police Officer with a healthy ego, but I still needed a letter like that. I needed to be praised for my work. It was dangerous, like all undercover operations. But I did it, and to have my big boss recognize my efforts meant a whole lot to me. Our players need to be praised when they deserve it. Our players need to be appreciated both as players and as people.

Praise is attitude and effort based, never exclusively performance based. Every practice, every conditioning session, every lifting day is an opportunity for our players to earn praise. When we as coaches look to lift others, we will find that inspires them to greater effort. The end result will be tangible improvements to our program.

A pitcher and infielder writes of how her coach went beyond words of praise to the demonstration of support and compassion:

> I had some major highs in my career but I also had some really low lows. Regardless of what it was, everything that ever happened, my coach was right there to either tell me he was proud of me or tell me

we'd get through it. The thing that showed me that I was cared about early on but most memorable was freshman year when my grandma, who I was really close to, passed away. When I got to the funeral I walked around to look at the flowers that were sent and see all the people that cared about my grandma, and I came up to a really beautiful peace lily plant addressed from the team. This happened during the beginning of the season and it was certainly a busy time, but he took the time to send me and my family flowers to make sure I knew that I was cared for. I still have the peace lily in my house actually.

An All-Conference catcher instructs us about praise unrelated to performance or outcome: "While it feels good to get praised for a timely hit, a home run, a good catch, or a great throw, I don't think I'll remember those moments forever. BUT I'm certain I'll never forget the praise I received in front of my entire team about my character, my attitude, my work ethic, or my effort."

Life is made up of intangibles. Things like this player mentioned: character, attitude, work ethic, effort. These are things that don't show up on stat sheets. They are more noble goals than a high batting average or a low earned run average. These are the qualities she will carry with her when her senior season is over. Long after anyone can remember her fielding percentage, they will recall what a great human being she was. Praise these qualities, and reward her with expressed appreciation.

A former professional player and All-Conference pitcher speaks of the consistency of her coach when it came to giving praise and appreciation:

> It was really no specific instance, but more so all of the time. Whether he needed me to come in as relief on the mound or come in as a DH, I knew that he counted on me. If you were "on" that game, he would definitely let you know it. The air fist bumps, the high fives in between innings, and the hand signals were all I needed. He would go around and praise every player like they were the best one to ever walk on the field, even if you had the worst game ever. I hope everyone gets a chance to play and learn from someone like him, both on and off the field … forever grateful.

An All-Big Ten shortstop tells how her coach found ways to appreciate her even when things weren't going so well on the field:

> The most memorable way my coach ever expressed her praise and appreciation for me was the way she always turned a negative situation into a positive one. It is very easy to be appreciated when everything is going good, but as we all know softball is a game of failure. The way she invested extra time in me whether it was watching film,

Chapter 5. Praise and Appreciation

taking more reps, or having the confident conversation with me to keep going, made me feel more appreciated than I ever have. No matter what the outcome was for the weekend, she was always there and when she couldn't be (because of time restrictions), she made it known she was still there for advice. She changed my outlook during tough times and made me realize the little victories in situations. This showed how much she respected and appreciated me and the game, pushing me to be the best athlete I could be.

Even the most stoic among us may express our appreciation for great achievements, but this wise coach wasted no opportunity to build her players up, even in the midst of failure.

An All-Region infielder with a national championship under her belt describes her coach's wise use of praise and appreciation:

> It would be easy to say that the most memorable way our coach expressed his praise and appreciation was in the final game of the 2019 National Championship as we held the school's first National Championship trophy proudly, but reality is, it's something that my teammates and I witnessed every day from our coach through his words and actions. As a team, we were reminded every day why we were recruited to be a part of a winning program. We were reminded that we were recruited based off of our hearts as people and not necessarily our talent as an athlete. Our coach was always sure to remind us of how grateful he was for us, because without us he wouldn't be able to do what he is so passionate about doing—coaching, teaching, and loving his athletes. His praise came in the form of tough love and we were always sure to "put it in our pocket" when we were given praise. Even in the midst of his tough love, we ALWAYS knew he was proud of us and we never once questioned it. We knew the motive of his coaching philosophy was to make us better people, better athletes, and to prepare us to win a National Championship.

It is interesting that she and her teammates were cognizant of her coach's coaching philosophy, one in which the first goal was to make them better people. Because he communicated his love through both tough love and praise, the appreciation he conveyed had great meaning.

A player from the same program joins in to affirm how her coach expressed appreciation in small but powerful ways:

> To me, the most memorable ways my coach expressed his praise and appreciation were the small gestures he would make. He wasn't one to sing your praises all the time, and we didn't need him to. When

Coaching Women's Softball

> he took the time to tell you that you had a good game or when he would send a text saying he was proud of you, you knew that you had earned it. Those small compliments meant the world to me. I would rather receive praise when I have earned it rather than being filled up with empty words conveying a false sense of skill and accomplishment. I don't think he knows how much it meant to me every time he sent me a text or called me after a game to tell me good job or that he was proud of me. These instances meant so much to me and all of my teammates because of how much we all respected him. He has his own special way of showing his praise and appreciation for his players and I will always be grateful for the times he expressed this to me.

This player alludes to a key component of the praise they seek. It absolutely must be authentic and truthful. Anything less will be sniffed out and read as manipulative.

A catcher from this same National Championship team adds to the picture of their very special coach:

> Our coach has a "tough love" mindset, at least on the field, and for me that was fitting. I grew up in a household with the same mindset and I knew I could handle pretty much anything he threw at me. Coach and I have a very unique relationship in ways that we can have a knock down drag out over something we are both passionate about and then tell each other we love each other minutes later. There are very few times Coach just hands out high fives or "atta baby's" and I respect him for that because I'm a firm believer in "not everything deserves a trophy." One specific time I remember, Coach was praising me is during our Conference Tournament my senior year. I led the game off with a home run on a pitcher that gave us the fits usually every time we faced her, but that wasn't a huge deal yet. Of course, he gave me a high five as I came around third, but it was what happened later on in the game that I'll never forget. A few innings later, I'm up again, this time bases are loaded. By the grace of God, I send the ball to deep left field and over the fence … a grand slam. As I rounded third base, Coach almost knocked my helmet off my head he was so excited!! I have never seen that man get so pumped up with me and although I might have had a slight concussion (kidding), that is a moment I will never forget. There are so many times I could continue to go on and on about how our coaching staff loved us and were always in our corner, but I may be writing my own book at that point! No words can truly express my experience with college softball, but I do hope that these short paragraphs give you a glimpse of the experience myself and so many others had there.

Chapter 5. Praise and Appreciation

An All-Conference utility player and designated hitter from this program, this Academic All-American recounts the words of praise that she carries with her years later:

> During my time playing for him there were many times that Coach expressed his praise and appreciation. There was always praise for the doing the little things, like a great situational hit, through encouraging words or a clap. For every home run I was praised coming around 3rd base. Over the five years that I threw batting practice to our team at every practice. Most people do not understand why I want to throw batting practice to my team every day as I was throwing 300–400 pitches a day. But I loved to serve my team and I saw it as part of my role in helping my team. There were many times over the years that Coach would tell me thank you for throwing batting practice and made sure I knew he was appreciative of it.
>
> But the most memorable way Coach expressed his praise and appreciation was at our senior appreciation party in 2017. Following a four-game sweep over one of our biggest competitors in the conference we had a senior appreciation party held by our parents. During the celebration the seniors were presented with our gifts from our parents at the front of the room. At this time Coach spoke to each of the seniors. When he got to me, he began to thank me for the service to the team and praise me for my ability to be a good teammate. He also praised my work ethic and passion for the game and the softball program. This led to tears from myself, Coach, and my family. This is the most memorable way Coach expressed his praise and appreciation as it was an acknowledgment of my ability to serve the program and my teammates outside of my athletic accomplishments. My goal entering college athletics had always been to be a good teammate before anything else and this was an acknowledgement of my accomplishment of that goal. This is one of the best memories I have from my time on the team.

A final player from that championship program relays a time when her coach paid her unforgettable words of praise:

> Personally, the most memorable way Coach expressed his praise and appreciation was a couple years ago when he nominated a couple of us to be a part of an organization on campus. He said something along the lines of him hoping his daughters grow up to be like us. I have never received such a high compliment as this, especially from someone I have the utmost respect for. I was stunned for Coach is not one to give out praise lightly. So it definitely meant that much more.

Coaching Women's Softball

> The praise and appreciation he gave was more often than not to others about us. He would have these "proud dad moments" where he would talk about us to other coaches or our families or whoever. And that was when we could see his love for us and passion for the program.
>
> Coach speaks and thinks so highly of his players, because he knows we are genuinely good human beings. But he wouldn't know that if he didn't make the conscious effort to get to know us as someone other than a softball player. That's the difference.

By expressing the thought that he hoped his daughters would grow up to be like her, this coach was giving her respect and admiration she would never forget.

A two-time NFCA All-American Scholar Athlete and NJCAA Division I National Championship team catcher speaks to the timing and context of the praise she received from her coach. This wise coach used practice time to use praise to reward effort:

> My coach gave praise and appreciation when I needed it, not necessarily when I wanted it. Rather than giving it right after a game winning hit or play, this praise was usually given during batting practice or through a discussion of my concerns about what I considered my "struggles." He infused confidence in me during these moments with positive reinforcement of what I was doing right while also providing constructive criticism to become better in the task at hand. Because of these moments, I never questioned his belief in me when I stepped in the box during any game situation. The confidence I had in him as a coach and the confidence he had in me as a player made the appreciation mutual, which played a significant role in my individual achievements and our success as a team.
>
> I also felt his appreciation through his trust in me as a catcher and pitch caller. He rarely questioned my decisions during a game and always offered suggestions when needed. He even let me call pitches while I was playing first base so another catcher could get experience behind the plate. This was an unspoken praise and appreciation I felt as he trusted me to get the job done.

This coach understood that praise and expressed appreciation is foundational for an athlete's confidence. We all know that confidence is essential to success in sports. Unlike many, this coach knew that praise is necessary if confident players are what we desire. An All-American outfielder from this same program describes her coach as intentional about loving his players and earning their love by his thoughtful actions:

Chapter 5. Praise and Appreciation

My respect for my JUCO coach started before I even met him—hearsay from players before me. He had a good reputation in the softball community. It didn't take long to understand for myself what kind of man and coach he was. He was open to us about his love for God and his family, and he treated each of us like his own. In doing so, I grew to respect him as I would my own parent. His expectations of me were clear both on and off the field. He was a coach I cared to make proud and tried not to disappoint. Not every coach earns that level of respect from their player, but Coach was definitely one for me.

I learned as many (or more) life lessons from him as I did softball lessons. He emphasized the importance of studies first, softball second. He taught us to be strong, independent women. He empowered us to see our value and frequently spoke to our individual strengths in order to build us up. He met each player right where they were. He got to know us on a personal level in order to know our needs. Some needed tough love and a loud voice to get motivated. Others, like myself, needed words of affirmation and a pat on the back to get motivated.

It is no coincidence that this team was the 2008 JUCO National Champions and 2009 runner-up. Notice the active verbs used to describe the love of this coach. She uses words like "empowered," "taught," "spoke to our strengths," and "got to know us to know our needs." This is the type of love in action that we would be wise to emulate.

An assistant coach has great opportunities to praise the athletes on the team. The assistant's role is often more informal and lends itself to encouragement, praise, and verbal appreciation. This Conference Player of the Year speaks of the impact of an assistant coach:

> Our former assistant coach had some of the most memorable ways of expressing her praise and appreciation for me. During practices my freshman and sophomore year we'd scrimmage on occasion and she'd be coaching third base while I was playing shortstop. I would make a play that I thought nothing special of, and she'd always say something like, "Hey, I sure do love to watch you play shortstop." Anytime I would make a mistake and hear about it, she did a great job of keeping me from losing confidence by simply counteracting it and saying something positive to me that made me feel someone believed in my abilities.

An All-American shortstop tells of how her coach went above and beyond to see that she was recognized and appreciated. The two-time conference player of the year and holder of the highest batting average among active Division II players explains:

Coaching Women's Softball

One of the most memorable ways Coach expressed his love and appreciation towards me personally was by sending in a story to News Channel 5 about my high school and college softball career. They did a "Curtain Call" for me on TV and I was overwhelmed with emotions. I do not play for the accolades. I play for my girls and my coaches. However, it was an awesome gesture that he did to show his appreciation for what I have done.

One of the most memorable ways Coach expresses his love and appreciation towards the team is just by being there for us, on and off the field. He is constantly checking in with us to see how we are doing in school, how our families are, where our mental state is at, etc.... He is constant and that has brought us closer together as a family!

A first baseman tells of her high school coach who expressed appreciation by her actions as well words. By assigning leadership responsibilities to her, this coach was praising her character and building her confidence:

My senior year of high school, we got a new head coach. I had never been coached by a female softball coach until that time. She was young and she played college ball. That was one of the most memorable seasons I've ever been a part of. We finished 3rd in the state that year. It wasn't because of the success that she stood out in my mind. It's the way she came into her very first year ever coaching with such confidence. She expressed her praise and appreciation for me not by telling me good job when I did something, but letting me have a big role in leading the team. She would text me things to get the girls to do, because she knew they looked up to me and she wanted certain things to come from players. She allowed me to play a big role in leading practices, team activities, and some big team decisions. I wish she would've been my head coach for longer, because she really knew and understood the game and all aspects of it.

For this All-Conference outfielder, her coach's words of praise at awards ceremonies were meaningful and memorable, especially since he recognized her classroom achievements as well as the athletic ones: "The most memorable way Coach showed his appreciation for me was during awards ceremonies he gave honest and detailed praise for my achievements both on the field and in the classroom. That made me feel so proud especially in front of my parents and peers. Coach was always talking to us which included giving us praise, but also giving us constructive criticism, both of which I needed then and always will!"

Chapter 5. *Praise and Appreciation*

An All-Conference third baseman tells how praise and confidence can be delivered in small, creative ways:

> In college we had this assistant coach who always had snacks and candy. If we got a trivia question right or had a great play we got a starburst. He would even slide us a starburst when we made it to first base. After a home run, the next day at practice we would get a box of candy in recognition. While its simple to say that we were "rewarded" for our good plays with candy, it was actually much more than that. Even if your bat was cold or you made an error and were beating yourself up, this coach would encourage you with a piece of candy. It was as if he was saying, "It's ok, you're still a great player, you've got this." Words are encouraging, but those simple handouts of candy meant more than words could ever say—both in celebration and encouragement.

As coaches we are obviously not professional therapists or experts in psychology, yet we inherit not only an athlete but often a wounded person with issues that are buried in a place we will never go. What we can do is to rebuild some of what was lost along the way with praise, appreciation, and affirmation. An All-Region pitcher references her personal baggage and her need for affirmation: "I feel like a lot of times I would play more for acceptance and to make people proud of me, which stems back from personal baggage issues from my relationship with my dad I think. Which I feel like most everyone's (especially girls) reasons for playing and the things that inspire us and drive us all come from how we have been treated and what we are hung up about from the past." These are gaps we can fill with praise and expressed appreciation. Though we don't know or necessarily need to know what issues may exist in some players from their pasts, a word of recognition praising their efforts can affirm them well beyond athletic accomplishments.

We can affirm and appreciate our players in another way: by listening to them. Instead of constantly speaking, listen. Our players have observations we may have missed and insights we may not have. Listen simply, for the respect and courtesy we are displaying when we stop talking, and listen with sincerity.

We might think we are listening to our players, but they may not think so. In response to the statement: "If I approach him/her respectfully, my coach will listen to my suggestions," 20 percent marked "False." Though 80 percent felt that statement was true, that we are listening, it also means that we turn away one in five, even though they are approaching us in the right way.

Coaching Women's Softball

A first baseman tells of the necessity of praise and affirmation, even for someone like her who was a three-time All-American and led the nation in home runs: "Each of my coaches who have ever made a difference in my life expressed their praise and appreciation by letting me know how good I was. They were always picking me up when I was down. They believed in me even when I didn't, and they made our whole team feel like we were the best team around. They never tore us down or spoke negatively about any of us. I found that a coach that builds us up creates a strong team, and a better bond between the coach and the athlete."

We may think that superstars like this player need less of our praise, but her testimony is that she needed a great deal of it. If anyone should have realized just how great she was, it should have been her. On the contrary, she craved affirmation and needed someone that would tell her how good she was.

Ironically, in some cases the current generation of high school and college young athletes have had too much undeserved praise heaped upon them. When coaches use praise when none is warranted, the athlete can become immune, and praise loses its power to improve and develop the athlete.

Former Bucknell Head Coach Courtnay Foster is currently the Associate Head Coach at UAB. She speaks of the overuse of praise as well as its proper use as a tool for improvement:

> It seems that the millennial generation has been conditioned to *expect* to be praised instead of *appreciating* praise when given. One reason for this is that praise is often a purely result driven and constant reality. How many times have you heard a parent or teammate say, "good job!" or "nice try" when it is not a good job at all? Or the contrary, have you heard a coach criticize or correct a player when there is improvement that falls just short of the end goal? I think that praise, when understood to reinforce *development*, is a valuable tool to create confidence and gratitude. Celebrating players working to seek and execute adjustments gives them the skills to self evaluate their performance and act on it, rather than only judging it as good or bad. This reduces reliance on external acknowledgement and promotes self-accountability which leads to results!

In other words, we need to evaluate carefully just exactly what it is we are praising. The player who refuses to make the adjustments at the plate we have made clear to her, yet still hits a game-winning double, may be

Chapter 5. Praise and Appreciation

undeserving of praise and appreciation. The pitcher to whom we teach a new change-up, and who gets a home run hit off of her trying to throw it correctly, is clearly deserving of praise. The outcome is unimportant; it is the intent that counts here.

Though we may seek as coaches to stay in the positive, ultimately our role is that of a teacher, and a teacher must make corrections. We obviously must deliver correction to our team on a regular if not daily basis, but the question is how are we going to proceed with it? If we can couch our corrective words without inducing feelings of isolation and broken connections, it is possible to reach them. While we may prefer to simply say what needs to be said in a concise and accurate fashion, we may be wasting everyone's time at best, and reducing chances for future success at worst.

I realized the importance of affirmation and encouragement in something as brief as the in-game pitcher conference. Like most coaches, if my pitcher was struggling during an inning or had lost her way, I would ask for time out and spend a few seconds with her to try to right the ship. The question was, how was I going to spend this valuable twenty seconds? What was my message for her? I knew what message I would want to hear if I were in her position, and I knew from coaching males what would work the best for them. I would want a short critique of what I was physically doing wrong and a sure tip to fix it ASAP. I might also respond to a challenge issued by the coach to get it together. But how should I approach her if I wanted the maximum benefit from the short conversation?

I learned quickly that what she was not looking for was a technical correction in her pitching motion, even if one was needed. This was not the time to teach or correct. She was also not seeking a rebuke or veiled threat of getting pulled from the game. What was most effective and had the highest percentage chance of success was to verbalize my confidence in her, thereby reassuring her that our connection was strong regardless of her performance. The visit was made even more successful when the infielders huddled around her for a couple of seconds, showing their support and helping her realize she was not isolated from her team in her struggle.

Once we determine the "what" we wish to praise, we must examine the "how." Anson Dorrance, Head Coach University of North Carolina Women's Soccer and 1986 USA Olympic Women's Soccer Coach, has written extensively on the subject of coaching female athletes and certainly has a track record of success on the field. With over 800 wins and

22 NCAA Women's Soccer Championships, he has accomplished things perhaps no other coach of female athletes has in any sport. He cautions coaches to be cognizant of the impact on the team at large when one player is singled out to be publicly praised: "Praise has to be doled out differently. Men love public praise, but if you praise a young woman publicly, every woman in the room now hates her with a passion, and every woman in the room also hates you, because you have not praised her. To top it off the young woman you praised hates you for embarrassing her in front of her teammates. However, a sincere and well-timed individual comment such as 'You were awesome' can be very effective and meaningful for any player."

While we should all be aware that criticism of an individual delivered in front of the whole team is a bad idea, singling out an individual to be praised in front of the group can also backfire. I remember a post-game talk after a tough split to a conference opponent. Our star pitcher, an All-Conference workhorse, had not pitched well in game one and seemed distracted. She failed to display her usual hyper-competitiveness and a less talented opposing team had a day against her. In the wrap-up after finishing the double header, the pitcher who won game two for us was complimented on her performance. Nothing negative was spoken of performance of the pitcher who struggled in game one. This one line of praise for the pitcher of game two set off a cascade of hurt feelings and drama through the team. Some of the team came to the side of the wounded pitcher, citing that the coach had been cruel in somehow inadvertently comparing the two. That division lingered throughout the year and caused animosity between teammates and especially between the two pitchers.

So, we see that giving players the praise and recognition they seek and deserve can be a tricky proposition. We must be careful to praise effort, attitude, and compliance with our instruction. Outcome alone can be influenced by luck or the failure of an opponent and is a poor driver of praise. We deliver the praise to all that deserve it, yet our words are chosen carefully so as not to invite comparison with the performance of other players. We have to be ever aware of the social dynamic, of how the words directed at one player will impact the other members of the team. What is important is not our words, but how those words are heard and understood.

Given all of these parameters and considerations to simply make a comment commending a player, we may be tempted to discontinue expressing praise altogether. That not being an option, we must instead

Chapter 5. Praise and Appreciation

improve our game when it comes to praising and appreciating our players. With some thought, we can become proficient at this, and in the process become a more positive and appreciative coach. Ultimately, as long as our praise is sincere and delivered with authenticity, it will be well received and effectual.

Chapter 6

Controlling Selfish Players

Perhaps we should define selfish players before we go any further. What we are not talking about are normal, competitive athletes with normal levels of concern over personal statistics and playing time. The true selfish player is one who takes self-promotion to a new level, resulting in negative consequences for the team at large. These are toxic teammates, with the potential to bring the entire program down if they are not checked.

Selfish players stir the pot in a variety of ways, but the result is always the same. Competition between pitchers on a softball team can be a powder keg of jealousy, sniping, and even sabotage. One of the pitchers I coached in college was extremely talented but unfortunately was all about her own stats and recognition above all else. I really believe that it was her desire that the other pitchers on the team fail miserably so that she would stand out as the "Number 1" pitcher in the rotation. I began to notice that whenever she was brought in the game as a relief pitcher (with runners on base), the first or second pitch would be hit for an extra base hit, clearing the bases of runners. These runners who scored would count against the previous pitcher, causing her Earned Run Average (ERA) to rise. What she did was to throw a "meat ball" to run up her teammate's ERA, plain and simple. After this, she would typically pitch very well for the rest of the game, usually dominating the other team.

This type of behavior is anything but rare based on survey results and by examples such as this one recounted by a former Division I pitcher:

> I had a third baseman, who if a ground ball was not hit directly in front of her, she would wait for the ball to get even with her feet and then dive over the ball instead of taking a side step to field the routine play. She did this to any play that required her to move side to side as to not chance an error. She knew if she made a diving effort the team

Chapter 6. Controlling Selfish Players

statistician would not count an error on her. This made it very hard as a pitcher because my goal became not only achieving ground balls for my defense, but also a ground ball not to third. We lost several games because of her selfish actions, and the team began to play as individuals rather than a unit, because they lost hope in success.

An NFCA West All-Region pitcher paints a picture of what it is like to have a selfish, toxic player on your team:

> I had a former teammate that was undoubtedly the most selfish athlete I have ever played with. Saying that, I now know and understand a lot of what was going on during that time. My feelings about this person have changed a lot. I spent 3 years on a team with this athlete. They made selfish decisions that could have ruined our seasons. They made blatant statements about their effort that was put forward, that they didn't care what happened especially when she didn't feel like giving full effort. They made statements about teammates with no care that they might have a negative impact on their teammate. This teammate did not care about anyone's feelings or what impact their selfishness had on the outcome of our seasons. The toughest part was that this teammate was extremely talented, constantly praised, and had a solid friendship with our coach. I feel like the coach saw a lot of the negative, but did not do much to help the situation because we were getting by with a lot of wins. The coach just tried to keep this teammate happy. I did have decent moments with this teammate, but I held a lot of frustration because I was very passive and nonconfrontational. I used to feel the same way the coach did, I just tried to keep this teammate happy honestly because I wanted to win, I wanted her to care, and I didn't want to be on her bad side. She was intimidating, blunt, controlling, and rude. We have a different relationship now. We are friendly with each other and she is much more authentic and caring. I believe that she is still who she is, blunt and carefree with words, but I feel like she understands the impact of words more and understands she needs community and commonality with others.

The description this pitcher gives of this disruptive player fits all athletes of this personality type. Statements such as "they made selfish decisions," "didn't feel like giving full effort," "did not care," "intimidating, blunt, controlling and rude" apply to most individuals who assume the role of the typical toxic player.

The coach joined many other coaches in the same position. She chose to placate, submit to, and pedestalize this undeserving athlete, simply because "We were getting by with a lot of wins."

Coaching Women's Softball

An All-Region PAC 12 catcher speaks of the body language selfish players utilize to signal their poor attitude: "The most common way a selfish player negatively impacted our team was through their body language. Body language is constant and contagious. Selfish players reacted to personal strikeouts, bad calls, errors, poor performances, or any undesirable outcome of that matter. Even subtle cues like an athlete's stance, look in the eye, sends a message to the opposing team, yes, but more importantly your own team." The former Team USA player contrasts two very different coaching responses to the antics of a selfish player: "My favorite coach created a culture that embarrassed anyone who acted that way, making it possible for players and coaches to keep each other accountable for the good of the team. My least favorite coach turned his head to this behavior because it was too uncomfortable for him, making it confusing for players to address these issues with each other. What was the standard?"

This kind of behavior is difficult to believe, but as coaches of female athletes, we must be aware of it. This selfish behavior is very difficult, maybe even impossible to change. Thankfully, most of your players are supportive of their teammates but you will certainly have a percentage of players who are not. It is difficult to prove their intentions, so our best defense against the damage it brings is to limit her opportunities to hurt the team. These athletes are often narcissists, which makes resolution of issues nearly impossible. Trying to mediate the damage they inflict with their hyper-selfish behavior can be the greatest challenge we face as coaches. Resolving conflicts between the selfish player and the rest of the team, including coaches, is a frustrating endeavor and often impossible. As is the case with other narcissists, the athlete characterized by an obsession with self-promotion coupled with a complete lack of empathy or remorse is a handful to manage. She actually can become worse if you come to her with concessions, as she will interpret your actions as weak and submissive. If you apologize in any sense, she will become more empowered as she claims victory over you. Worst of all, these players are often charismatic, and their insubordinate attitude holds a certain allure to other players on the team. They often have a significant following and corresponding negative influence. They will spin your attempts to correct their behavior, and your actions will be misrepresented so that you as a coach appear to be the bad guy.

Our response to the selfishness of such narcissistic players must be immediate, fair, and unwavering. Decisiveness is the key to dealing with the habitually selfish player. You must know going into battle with one

Chapter 6. Controlling Selfish Players

of these that you are ready and willing to expel her from the team if she doesn't comply with your standards of conduct and behavior. This is the only way to maintain a chance of her remaining with your program. She will not like being forced into a submissive role one bit, but there are no other options. More than likely she has never been stood up to before by parents or coaches, and she probably will not take it lying down. If she agrees to comply with your demands, expect her to do so reluctantly and barely. Expect her to cross the line again, and be prepared to meet that defiance with expulsion if warranted. Our overarching mindset with habitually selfish players must be that we will not allow them to bring the program down. They will be removed from the team before they do so. No matter their stats, we must take a step back and realize that they just aren't worth it.

An All-Region outfielder and NFCA Scholar Athlete tells of the toxic impact of one selfish teammate, and the fair but firm manner in which her coach dealt with such behavior:

> One year I was on the team I played with a girl who didn't like to uphold the guidelines that my head coach put in place. She was constantly breaking curfew, hanging out around the wrong crowd and getting in trouble, with not only the team but with the University. This became a bigger issue when she was influencing other girls on the team to participate in the bad habits she was falling into. Our team culture began to falter because our softball program is built on integrity, selflessness, hard work, and discipline. Our team began straying away from these characteristics and it all stemmed from this one player who was being selfish and bringing the team down with her. Coach teaches us discipline more than anything and when she is faced with situations such as this one, she calls a meeting with them to have an intentional talk with her player to get to the bottom of the problem. She is not the type of coach to immediately give up on her players; she believes in grace and forgiveness—which attests to her being a Christian coach. However, if the player doesn't show signs of wanting to buy into the culture that has been built and feels as though they are negatively affecting the team, she will have a conversation with them about not being the right fit for the program. I have so much respect for the way Coach handles things because she truly cares about her players as people first and athletes second.

A former All-Conference pitcher tells of how selfish players fragment and undermine teams: "My experience with selfish players has led me to realize one player can truly change the team dynamic. When a player is more worried about themselves, the team immediately splits. Two things can happen: the team isolates the player, causing drama, or the focus of the team turns towards the player instead of the goal of winning. Both ways can spiral out of control quickly."

This pitcher made an important observation when she realized that one player can change the whole team's dynamic. When distrust is created between players and between players and coaches, precious energy is expended by everyone involved. Distracted by the drama that follows, the team loses its edge, and success becomes unattainable. One thing is certain: your team is watching to see how we handle this disruptive individual. Are we strong enough to face her down, regardless of what she brings to the table athletically? Or will we hide our heads in the sand, hoping she will eventually change? What happens when a player, especially an All-Conference one, defies us as coaches? The team has their popcorn and are eagerly watching our performance.

The two approaches mentioned by this insightful pitcher are equally ineffective. If the team shuns or isolates the selfish player, the player will intensify her efforts to regain her power. In an attempt to win the war against her teammates, she will enlist the support of parents and school administrators. Expect to receive scathing emails from her parents and inquiries from the college president or high school principal.

Her resolve to cause problems will intensify as she targets a few players on the team. The claws will come out, as she publicly slanders a couple of players and one of the coaches. The narcissist in her cannot deal with being ignored.

The other option mentioned is the team gives the selfish player the attention she craves, focusing on her rather than on winning games. She can become center stage, the main topic of conversation between players, and the reason you can't win.

A standout catcher explains how one player changed an entire season, actually sabotaging her team at NCAA Regionals and effectively ruining their season: "We lost regionals. A negative teammate that didn't 'buy in' lost us our shot at continuing on. All season long this teammate questioned everything we did. She tried to get us to question what our coach had us doing and how much our coach really knew. Earlier in the season she had been beat out of her position and it all went downhill from there."

The incident at Regionals that this catcher describes was a demonstration of selfishness that was actually difficult to fathom. I watched as this player threw a hand grenade on the dreams of an

Chapter 6. Controlling Selfish Players

entire team. She had been a starter the prior season, but now in her junior year had been beaten out of her starting role. Relegated to the role of a pinch runner, her resentment festered throughout the season. She grumbled her discontent through the regular season, directing her negative comments towards the player who supplanted her as well as the coach who made that decision. In spite of her selfish attitude, nobody seemed to buy into her misery. The team had a great year, fighting through the losers' bracket in the Conference tournament to emerge the champions, winning in dramatic fashion with a walk-off home run in the ninth inning.

The player immediately voiced her disappointment that the season was extended by being crowned conference champions. In the midst of a joyous celebration over winning the conference tournament, this player was sullen and angry.

As we began play at NCAA Regionals, it appeared that this player was not going to impact our success. We drew a top-ten team from the West Coast in our first game and lost a very even 1–0 game. Rallying back, we run ruled the other team our next game and advanced to face off in a rematch with our first game opponent. This time our players brought their best and won a one run game, shocking the California team.

Heading into game four, we knew we had our hands full, facing the hosting team, a perennial Division III powerhouse. By the middle of the game, we were holding our own, trailing by one run. Our number three batter was up and managed a hit up the middle. Calling time out, the head coach substituted our disgruntled selfish player to pinch run at first base. With two outs and our All-American short stop (who led all of Division III in home runs) up, we knew this was our chance. On the first pitch, our batter blasted a towering shot to left field that cleared the fence by forty feet. From my spot in the first base coaching box, it wasn't the home run I noticed; it was our runner blatantly and obviously intentionally leaving first base early. During the windup she sprinted from first and was four steps towards second base by the time the pitcher released the ball. Worse yet was that one of the two field umpires was positioned behind first base and observed the infraction unfold before him. As our team and our fans screamed in excitement as our runners rounded the bases, they failed to notice the umpire at first base signaling the out for leaving early. As the noise died down, everyone realized that the home run was null and void, and that our inning was over with our runner causing the third out. The air went out of the team as they realized their chance to win this game was gone, their one opportunity stolen by a disgruntled, selfish player. This player took away this special team's season, and their hopes to advance to the World Series.

This insightful catcher explains the behavior of selfish players and how they distract a team: "Selfish players are there to draw attention to themselves no matter positive or negative, most of the time negative. These people want to distract and discourage everyone, and they want the team to think twice about all of the hard work they are putting in. To me, they seem to be on the team for all the wrong reasons. In choosing to ignore the negative person, you are choosing to believe in your team; you are choosing to 'buy in' to the program."

A conversation I had with a college coach about an NCAA Regional game I watched reveals the negative impact a self-centered player brings to the field. Going into the game, his team was anticipating a battle because the pitcher on the opposing team was a two time All-American. It didn't take long until this coach and his team gained the upper hand as they watched the selfish pitcher snipe at her teammates and disrespect her coach. The coach saw this behavior as the destructive to the entire team, and his team was energized by the havoc this All-American was causing to her own team. His team defeated what was perhaps a more talented team with a superstar pitcher due to one player's selfishness. His team went on to win that Regional, the Super Regional, and the College World Series. He credits this selfish player for giving them the win and the opportunity to progress toward their goal.

If only it were possible to ignore the selfish player among us. As difficult as it is to deal with them, our players are looking to us to confront and redirect the selfish, team-destroying player. An All-American first baseman recalls how the failure of coaches to deal with a selfish player impacted the team:

> I dealt with a selfish player in college. They were always late to practice and even warm-ups for games. There would be some days she wouldn't show up to practice at all and no one would know where she was. She would show up to our workouts in attire that didn't match the team and it distracted everyone. As a whole we were still successful, but it caused drama within the team and distracted everyone from our actual goal. We really had to focus and try not to let it bother us even though our coaches let her get away with everything. It made it hard for the team to think positively and distracted many of us from fully focusing on a successful season.

Chapter 6. Controlling Selfish Players

The fact that the team's perception was that "our coaches let her get away with everything" is particularly disturbing. The team observed the selfish, non-compliant behavior of this player, then watched as the coaches failed to confront her. Cowardice on the part of their coaches was seen as an endorsement of her defiance. Failure to act in these situations is the worst possible course of action. Stand up to selfish players. Make them comply like everyone else. The wearing of non-approved practice attire is a classic move by these narcissistic players. This player was actually wearing her defiance and by doing so proclaiming her dominance to the players and coaches. We simply cannot afford to take a passive approach to such selfish rebellion. We must meet the challenge brought by such players head on.

An All-Conference catcher tells how the selfish player can take the life out of a team: "Negativity is toxic. Instead of focusing on getting better and taking more reps, we were spending our energy trying to ignore her, pump her up, or engage with her in an effective way. Very depleting for the entire team."

An All-Conference pitcher describes how a selfish player detracted from the unity of the team. She even found herself wishing that this player would fail because she wasn't a true teammate: "Her actions and attitude took away from team camaraderie and our level of play as a whole. It made you not want them to do well because you knew they didn't have the investment in the success of the team that the rest of us had."

Emotional energy is a limited commodity on a team. When that energy is spent trying different strategies to deal with the toxic, selfish player, the entire team deflates. These players thrive on the attention as the different plans to deal with them are rolled out. "Pumping her up" will not work, as her massive ego is already overinflated. Engagement is impossible because this person uses people rather than forming bonds with them. Ignoring her will only prompt her to push harder against the boundaries. The selfish player must be met head on, and this is our responsibility, not the team's.

An outstanding infielder speaks of how one selfish player can destroy team focus:

> Selfish players are toxic to teams. Their acts draw the attention to themselves and away from the focus of the team, whether that is their intention or not. A team, as a whole, should be all in on the team focus and dedicated to the team and their goals. This requires every single

individual player to be all in. If there are 15 players on the team, and if 1 out of the 15 acts in a selfish way, then that can prevent a team from reaching full potential. A team being the best version of the team requires every single person on that team to make the CHOICE to commit to the team. Even if the remaining 14 are fully committed and act selflessly toward the team, that one person's selfish behavior draws attention away from the team focus.

When a player cares more about themselves than they do the team, it devalues the team. A team is a unit and can only function at max ability when the full team is in and loves those around them.

This player's summary captured the essence of the matter when she wrote, "Selfish players are toxic to teams." They are poisonous, carrying both long and short-term toxins. Though their toxicity may not be apparent at first, be sure that their impact will be felt eventually. Symptoms of toxicity are team underachievement, a high level of tension, and an inability to win on a consistent basis, especially against strong competition. Your selfish player will inject her venom and stand back and watch as it takes effect across your team.

We may not think that much damage is being done to our team by selfish team members, but the players see it differently. When presented with the statement: "Selfish players held my team back from being as successful as we could have been," 86 percent marked "True." Their perception is that this factor plays a major role in the success or failure of the team. In other words, selfish players undermine our coaching strategies and gut team unity. Selfish players diminish our success. They turn wins into losses. They rob the entire team of joy, of having a positive experience in what should be one of the most meaningful periods of their lives. They cause misery to the players we value and care about. They cause us to lie awake at night, they cause our blood pressure to rise, they are bad for our health. So why do we find ourselves reluctant to deal with them in a fair yet decisive manner?

The problem presented by a selfish "star" player becomes even more concerning. Our players feel that we as coaches too often grant special latitude to our star players. It is especially disturbing that 56 percent of our players think we are blowing it here, marking "True" to the statement: "The behavior of selfish star players was not checked and dealt with by my coach." In their eyes, we are owned by selfish program makers, losing our integrity in the process. Whether this perception is true or not, many of our players are convinced of it. The situation calls out for us to level the field and regain the respect we may have lost. Female

Chapter 6. Controlling Selfish Players

athletes can see through any pretense when it comes to treating some players differently than others. If we are making concessions to selfish star players, our team will sniff that out in no time.

Reflecting on her playing days, Birmingham Southern College Coach Kimball Cassady recalls how favoritism towards star players negatively impacted the team: "The worst I can remember is when our best players just wouldn't put the work in, yet they always got more reps and more attention. They were the suck ups that the coaches liked, but yet those players would complain and talk about other people and the coaches. These type players became hard to be around and hard to trust."

It is interesting that these players often ingratiate themselves to coaches, capitalizing on the value their on-field talent brings. As the survey confirms, we can be blind to the real nature of these talented but toxic players. Perhaps in our short sightedness, we have turned a blind eye to their schemes. Over half of our players think we have.

Texas Lutheran Head Coach Wade Wilson, 2019 Division III World Series champions, speaks to managing selfish players. He tells of having to remove a valued starter from the team just before the World Series due to the toxic impact of her selfishness:

> For those that have not coached a selfish player; is there such a thing? We have all coached selfish players, some more selfish than others. There are definitely degrees of selfishness. There is hope for these players if and only if you have a strong group around them that are selfless and able to correct and redirect selfish behaviors. If you have a team of selfish players, your days are numbered as a team. I tell our teams every year that the most talented team usually doesn't win the championship; it's the team that does the little things well, every time and selfless. Selfish players always show up at the most inopportune time, when you least expect it. More times than not the selfish players will eliminate themselves if the others do not tolerate their behavior(s).
> I have had to dismiss a player from a team one time in my career for being selfish; it is not an easy thing to do. We were in the playoffs and noticed that she was not all-in and did my best to just ignore it. I had a choice to either confront her or ignore it with hope that she would figure it out and enjoy the successes of her teammates. We made it through that weekend but when we returned I was approached by several of our leaders. They informed me that the entire team would rather not have her on our team the rest of the season; she was a distraction and a liability to what they were trying to accomplish. We

finished the rest of the season without her and didn't lose another game. It's hard to tell if this made a difference or not because we were able to overcome her selfishness the games leading up to that, but we were all pulling the rope in the same direction with her gone.

What Coach Wilson omitted was that he dismissed this player just before leaving for the Division III World Series. This great coach placed principles over pragmatism, removing a strong player because she was not in compliance with his team's core values. In a move that many would not make, he opted to remove a starter from the team who was instrumental in getting them to this point. He trusted in her replacement and in the rest of his players to make up for her loss, and they did. Coach Wilson's Texas Lutheran Bulldogs went on to win the 2019 Division III Championship, going 6–0 and out scoring their opponents 43–17.

Wade Wilson, 2019.

University of Tennessee Assistant Coach Megan Rhodes Smith relates her strategies for dealing with the selfish player. The former Vols standout pitcher who helped UT to three World Series appearances takes a deliberate approach, but tailors her response to the player and her situation:

> Controlling selfish players can truly be a chore. I've seen it done several ways, sometimes effectively and sometimes ineffectively. I haven't quite figured out which method is "most often effective" as I have seen the same method be both successful and unsuccessful depending on the athlete, the coach, and the situation.
>
> No matter what, I believe the coach must choose to act. Perhaps the

Chapter 6. Controlling Selfish Players

coach sits the athlete down and walks her through her behavior while pointing the athlete towards the better way. Perhaps the coach makes a big demonstration publicly in front of the team to make a point and maintain the trust of the team. Perhaps the coach spends a lot of time in team building or teaching character and lets the behavior die out on the athlete's time.

I have found that being direct, honest, and kind to be the route that resonates best for me, especially when dealing with an athlete who is, perhaps, not truly selfish but merely acting selfishly. I believe there is a difference between the two and that treating a person with dignity reminds them of who they ought to be in a more lasting and inspirational way than berating or shaming. Though some don't respond to this, I have found that the majority do and appreciate a coach who is willing to call out the good rather than shame the bad.

Perhaps one strategy we must employ is to preemptively exclude selfish players from our programs. Once they are a part of the program, it is difficult to sever them when the selfishness rears its head, and even when ties are cut, it is often messy and painful for all involved. Jacksonville State University Head Coach Jana McGinnis speaks of being careful to understand the person you are recruiting before you make an offer to them. By doing due diligence in the recruiting process, we may save ourselves from having to manage a selfish or disrespectful player later: "When recruiting young athletes, it is very important to get to know a player as much as possible. Talk to as many people as you can about the prospect. Living in today's world, we now

Megan (Rhodes) Smith, 2008.

have social media that we can look at in order to find out what is important to the prospect. You can learn fast if the athlete has respect for herself and others by what she posts on her social media."

While landing a five-star recruit can be exhilarating, we need keep our eyes wide open lest we open our team to the toxicity of a selfish player.

We need to understand that when coaching female athletes, selfish, toxic players must usually be dealt with by their coach. Intervention outside of the players' circle becomes necessary to shut down the impact of these players. When coaching males, this may not be the case. With male athletes, this is a problem that will often be handled within the team and by the players themselves. Males have a tendency to confront the selfish player, robbing them of any influence over the team. Especially as male coaches, we may recall from our playing days how such players were dealt with player to player. We should not expect that the same internal mechanism will take place on a female team.

So selfish players are a team problem that we alone are responsible for dealing with. Meeting the challenge of these who seek to infect our programs for their own benefit is one of our greatest coaching challenges. We can try different strategies, but ultimately, we will need to

Jana McGinnis, 2020.

Chapter 6. Controlling Selfish Players

meet these types head on and resolve the issue in the best interest of the team. Perhaps our best defense against the narcissistic player is to screen them out before they ever set foot on our campus. We must be prepared for the player who makes it through the recruiting undetected as a toxic, destructive player. With a strategy in place we meet this challenge, always placing the health of the team above the athletic contributions of this type of person. We know that others will be watching to measure our response to this dilemma. The team, your staff, and parents will observe as your stated values are tested, to see whether you will place your team above this selfish player.

Dealing with the destructive player, the narcissist, may be the biggest coaching challenge we face. How we face it will reveal a lot about us as coaches. Whatever the path we choose here, the impact on our team will run deep. We have the choice of what kind of impact that will be.

Chapter 7

Respect Is Everything

The worst thing that can happen in my mind is a lack of respect for the coach. Respect is a fickle idea. But, coaches should display full and total confidence in themselves and not waiver on their demands on and off the playing field. The best respect is certainly earned but also demanded. As a coach, you are in a position of authority and a position of leadership. It is your duty as the captain of your ship to make sure that you get out to sea and back successfully. Teach your players to row together and don't be afraid of appropriate punishment when they don't follow direction. In most cases, demanding best effort be given is a way to maintain top athletes' respect.
—All-Region outfielder and career .400 hitter

Everything coaches do and say should build and maintain the respect of their players. If there is correction to be given, it must be done in a way to maintain respect. If we curse our players, call them names, if we degrade or embarrass them in front of their teammates—we have lost their respect to some degree. If we are often out of control, if we consistently blow up on the field in anger during games—we are certainly in the process of losing their respect. Once respect is lost, we can no longer teach or coach because their hearts and minds are closed to us.

While respect for her coach as a person on and off the field is a cornerstone of the relationship between the female athlete and her coach, the male athlete looks predominantly at the ability to win as the determinant of respect. If his coach can win games and championships, males will overlook negative issues such as found in the "Bobby Knight" type of aggressive coach.

Karen Thatcher, a member of the 2010 U.S. Women's Olympic Hockey team, elaborates: "Embarrassing or degrading her in front of her teammates is the worst strategy with a female athlete. It does

Chapter 7. Respect Is Everything

not motivate the athlete to improve; instead, it encourages her to feel poorly about herself and may cause her to be fearful to even attempt to improve. Female athletes also tend to emotionally carry this type of experience along with them, leading to perhaps inhibiting her develop in the future as well. This strategy often causes more harm than good."*

I knew a coach, a very competent coach, whose career took him to several colleges as head coach. His tenure at each school normally ended badly, with him getting fired and moving on to another school. His problem wasn't that he couldn't coach, because he was extremely competent. He had a respect problem brought on by a temper that caused him to verbally and publicly abuse players who made him mad. He was doomed to failure by his own sharp tongue. When he did this to one player, he would lose the respect of the entire team. Not only did this reduce his talented squads (he was a great recruiter) to barely average teams, it cost him his career. His players banded together, determined not to perform for a coach they didn't respect. He still fails to take responsibility for his lack of control and blames "entitled" players for his fate.

I wish that the coach I just described was alone in having anger management issues that gutted his team's respect for him/her. I have witnessed embarrassing fits of rage by coaches during games, often at the college level. At the high school and club ball levels, I have seen some great coaches who sincerely loved their players sabotage themselves with an out-of-control temper.

This narrative about a coach who was undeserving of any respect whatsoever is told by a former All-Conference Utility player. The behavior of the coach may seem extreme, but it is not unheard of, unfortunately:

> My story about a time that I lost respect for a coach can be a bit of a difficult story other to hear so I apologize in advance, but it is real and raw. At my prior university I lost respect for my head coach to the point where I hated her tremendously. I was a full scholarship athlete and started nearly every game but me and 20 other young women were being abused on a daily basis. We were told we were stupid or fat, on the field frequently, and were punished for the most minor inconveniences. I could tell you an unlimited number of things that were done to me personally and my team, but I will only list few.
>
> At one point my team was demanded to run until there were 9 girls standing (what it takes to fill a roster) because she wanted those 9 women to start next game because this meant they "wouldn't quit." We ran until

---
* Amidon, "Coaching Strategies."

Coaching Women's Softball

near 12 of our teammates were on the ground, passed out on the floor with medical attention from a trainer, or vomiting. I believe that athletes should be pushed, not nearly injured. Our assistant coach quit his job immediately after this due to fear of legal repercussions, and our coach proceeded to tell us he was a quitter and soft. We were obviously scared. This was only one of dozens of borderline abusive conditionings we did.

Another instance we were traveling to Georgia for games and we drank all the waters on the bus. Our coach yelled at us and told us she would not be buying us any more water and that our parents couldn't bring us any. We were stuck without water for the rest of the 9-hour trip until we were able to get to our hotels and drink of out the faucets. On top of it we were often not allowed to see our families, had to give our phones to her and would run if were forgot to tuck in our shirts when we got off the bus on these trips.

Our coach would unannounced and uninvited walk into our apartments and yell at us if our trash was not taken out and infer that we were sluts if we had boys at our apartments, even if they were our boyfriends.

She controlled and shamed us over food choices.

Lastly, we had something called "field hours." One time I forgot a piece of paper she gave me in the locker room. When I returned to get the paper, I was given 20 hours of field work which had to be completed by the end of the week. The field hour tasks could be anything from field labor, to scrubbing bird poop off the backstop, to cleaning the locker room. We only had one week to complete these hours of work around school and softball. It didn't matter if you were there until 2 a.m. This was something she frequently did to us for anything and everything.

Every aspect of our lives was controlled, and due to living in this constant fear of repercussions for normal things, I developed an eating disorder to gain some control in my life, lost 20 lbs and began self-harming repeatedly. I was taken to a suicide ward in a hospital to be assessed and before I left to go my Coach told me if I want to play in the game the next day, I would need to be cleared by them. She inferred I should lie, so I lied when I was clearly suicidal, but I wanted to play.

As a current college coach now, I could never respect a coach who runs their program like this.

This story reminds us that our players all have their limits, and this cruel coach chipped away at this young woman's mind until she attempted to take her life. Leaving her to deal with an eating disorder and other suicidal behaviors, this coach left a legacy of destruction in this young person's mind. Who knows how many others she harmed by her sadistic behavior.

Chapter 7. Respect Is Everything

Thankfully this player's story has a second chapter, one where a kind and loving coach helped to heal her and turn her life around. While this player's first coach was worthy of no respect, her second college coach earned her respect and was able to lead her on the road back to a healthy mind and body:

> Now we will move onto the program and the coach that saved me from self-harm and gave me the experience I played softball my whole childhood for. When I finally decided to transfer and get myself out of that controlling and abusing player coach environment, my new coach was always there. He respected me and allowed me to explore my own transfer process while always having open arms for me. I came battered and broken and unable to understand this healthy softball environment I was in. I was mean to my teammates and didn't understand him. How he could let people laugh while they throw at practice, or how he could let someone tell him "ya" instead of "yes sir" without running. SOFT. My Junior year was rough, but he stuck with me through self-harm and softball injuries. My teammates did not understand the pain I was suffering and how could they. This was my mess to fix, but little did I know they would help mend the wounds.
>
> My senior year when my old coach was finally exposed and fired, I was able to move on and begin healing. I got professional help frequently and I started to understand who I was again. That I didn't want to hurt myself or others, I wanted to love my program as much as I loved softball. I became a better person, teammate and player. I began to trust my coaches and grew to love them. I could suddenly make and maintain relationships in my life which has led me to so many people I am grateful for.
>
> My coach has helped me secure my first college coaching position as a graduate assistant and I am currently getting my MS in Athletic Leadership. He has been an incredible mentor to me. My senior year was my savior in my life. I am now engaged and 4/6 of my bridesmaids are from my softball team, the other two are my biological sisters. All three of my coaches are invited to my wedding and I will continue to donate and volunteer to this softball program forever.

This story ended well. Certainly, there are others where the abuse went unchecked with tragic results.

An All-American infielder tells of another, more subtle form of abuse. She shares how a coach's comments about her weight affected her deeply. It informs us as coaches just how hurtful inappropriate comments about appearance can be. Though the words may be meant to

Coaching Women's Softball

motivate, they serve only to wound and discourage. As the words do their damage, the respect we need so desperately as coaches slips away:

> I have always struggled with weight. The only place I truly felt confident was the softball field. I knew I was talented and when I stepped on to the field I was more confident in that uniform than in my own skin in everyday life. Unfortunately, this all started to crumble right in the middle of my college softball career.
>
> It started off with small comments from my coach every now and then. These different comments consisted of things like walking in to get ready for practice eating baked Lays chips and him saying, "Glad to see you picked the healthy option today" or when he gave me an XXL in pants and said he didn't think I could fit into a smaller size instead of asking me what size I want like he did everyone else on the team. There were also times when we would travel for games and he would call me out on the bus in front of the entire team letting me know he brought plenty of snacks. These comments happened more and more often the entire year.
>
> This truly made me feel like nothing was possible at the weight I was. I was extremely discouraged and realized he only saw me based on looks and not based on talent. Luckily, I still ended up getting to play my senior season even though I had to deal with the constant comments about my clothing, what I ate, my speed, or the way I looked.
>
> Even though all of this occurred, I still choose to be proud of myself. I do not want him to be able to take anything else from me. My advice to current and future coaches is to think about what you are saying before you say it. Really get to know your athletes and treat them how they deserve to be treated. They work hard to perform at the highest level to the best of their abilities, and all they need from you is your support and knowledge to lead them to success. Tearing your athletes down will not make them better or bring them any closer to success.

An All-American shortstop tells of how a coach's post-game tirade resulted in a permanent lack of respect from her players.

> It was in the state championship game my senior year for softball. This was my very last game of my high school career. Score was tied 1–1 going into the middle of the 6th inning when a crazy incident happened that caused our game to be delayed for about 45 mins. While this delay was happening, the intensity of the game went away and my team was forced to stay on the field. Our pitcher got cold and everyone lost focus. There were already two outs in that inning before this incident happened. The first batter after the delay roped a double down the left field line. Our pitcher left it right over the heart of the plate.

Chapter 7. Respect Is Everything

The next batter was a slapper so I was pulled in to defend the short slap. The slapper hit a short pop up that landed on the edge of the grass right in front of our left fielder. She played it wrong and when it hit the ground, the ball spun all the way to the fence on the 3rd base side. This caused the go ahead run to score. We ended up losing the game 2–1.

After the end of the game, my team was in the dugout waiting to get the second place medals when my head coach comes into the dugout and starts cussing me out and saying I was the reason we lost the game. She was yelling so loud that the other players and even our parents in the stands could hear every word she was saying to me. But, the minute the headmaster of our school came onto the field to present the trophy and medals, she did a complete 180 and started praising everyone, especially me, about how well we played. That very exact moment is when I lost respect for her as a coach. She belittled me in front of everyone for two plays that I had no control over. I didn't touch the ball in that 6th inning. One player can't win a game or lose a game all by themselves. That's not how you coach. You don't chew out a player in front of everyone saying they lost the game for the rest of the team and then turn around and give praises to that player and the rest of the team. I lost respect for her as a coach and especially as a person. That's not the kind of coach or person I would want in my life. Coaches should be there to support you and also push you to do your best. Not to belittle you and blame the loss on one single player.

Failure to control our tempers, raging at players who are often innocent of any wrongdoing, is an automatic respect killer. It is bullying of the worst kind, where the players' subordinate position precludes fighting back. Those who witnessed the scene described above will likely never forget it, and they will most likely never respect that coach. Sadly, this coach didn't even have the decency to apologize when she cooled off.

Obviously, verbal communication plays a huge part in coaching. It is necessary to be vocal in a direct, passionate manner. We can get loud and intense at times. We have to say things to our players that are not always pleasant or welcomed. These are normal, necessary interactions between coach and player, and most players accept this. The anger generated speech that will drain your players' respect away is entirely different. We as coaches need to make sure that we understand the difference. If we do not, and continue to use what is simply verbal abuse as our go to, we need to be prepared for failure.

William Peace University Head Coach Charlie Dobbins talks of the fine line that divides having a competitive spirit and ugly aggression: "A common theme of every great coach is the will to win. Bring energy to everything you do to inspire your team forward. Be cautious that the 'will to win' does not spill over into aggression or the use of unethical methods to achieve victory. All wins should be always with class and sportsmanship."

Coach Dobbins suggests, "Bring energy to everything you do to inspire your team forward." Many in coaching lack any energy to bring, suffering from burnout. Characterized by a lack of positive energy and waning interest in the program, it is a major respect killer. In the burned-out coach, our players see one who has the knowledge and skills to help them succeed but lacks the enthusiasm to do so. The player enters her freshman year of college full of optimism and motivation but is met by a coach whose positive energy left years ago. Seeing the gap between their enthusiasm and the coach's, the team's respect for the authority of the coach erodes quickly. The attempts to motivate by a burned-out coach are hollow words, hype not backed up with any level of sincerity. The burned-out coach is often a disgruntled person, disappointed with their professional success and bitter against those whom they hold responsible for their lot in life. Such a coach has no business leading a team of young athletes who deserve much more. They deserve a coach who is enthusiastic and innovative. An inspiring person who approaches every season as an opportunity to not only coach players up but to love and mentor them. This is the kind of coach they are inclined to respect.

The ultimate respect killer for a coach is when accusations are made of an inappropriate relationship between coach and player. Far from being a rarity, the instances of coach-player physical involvement are far too commonplace. For a coach to engage with one of their players in this forbidden manner will not only rob the coach of all respect, it causes irreparable harm to the player and the team. Unfortunately, this type of behavior often goes on privately and undetected for a time. Whether or not the coach is called to account for their actions, the team will suffer harm from these indiscretions.

In order to avert any false accusations in this area, we as coaches must be circumspect in how we interact with players on the field and off. We must guard our reputations by adhering to guidelines that protect us from those who would destroy us with false accusations. As a male coach, I would not meet with a player, any player, alone. If I was having a private bullpen session with a pitcher, a catcher was present. If a player wanted to meet to talk or share personal concerns, we did so at a location on campus where there were people all around us. If I wanted to

Chapter 7. Respect Is Everything

meet with a player, I would always have either my head coach or at least another player present.

I made it clear early on that I was not a relationship coach and did not want to hear about their romantic relationships unless they wanted to report abuse. I never, ever commented on their weight, good or bad, leaving that to my female head coach if fitness issues needed to be addressed. I never commented on their appearance when, for instance, the team was dressed up for a softball banquet, unless I made a group-wide compliment. Of course, jokes or coarse jesting about sexual matters were off limits, as was any form of touching including assisting them in stretching. These protections should be self-evident, but I have witnessed all of these mistakes with grave consequences, giving credence to false accusations made.

Know that any private text you send that could be misconstrued will be circulated to other players. Though it may have been an innocent message, if taken out of context and embellished by player's commentary, it can be the undoing of the team's respect for you. Before we speak, show affection, text or post, we have to pause and ask, "How does this look?" If we proceed without thinking our actions through, it could mark the end of respect from our team, as well as our undoing as a coach.

The cause of a loss of respect can result not only from big issues like verbal abuse, improper relationship accusations, or dishonesty. We can also unintentionally lose the respect of a player by behavior that is not necessarily offensive or wrong. For example, depending on the background of a player, cursing in conversation can lower our status in their eyes. Similarly, cursing for effect after a loss or to make a point may seem harmless but can come across as crude and show a lack of class from the point of view of the team. If we as coaches do not allow filthy language from our players, we must hold ourselves to the same standard. Anyone can lose the reins on their tongue during the height of emotions, but those outbursts we have all had still need to be avoided or at least apologized for. We may think these are young adults that don't need to be shielded from rough language, but when respect is in the balance, we should consider avoiding the use of crude language if possible.

Another morally neutral behavior that can lower our status is drinking alcohol in front of or with our players. We must realize that some of the players on our team may come from a family background where alcoholism was a problem. These players may equate drinking of any magnitude with the destruction they have seen in their own history. Additionally, a player may be struggling with the abuse of alcohol in her own life. This is not to judge or to suggest that consuming alcohol is wrong. It is simply that drinking in view of our team could chip away at the respect players have for us.

One thing I learned when I began coaching in college was that my personal life, my family relationships, and manner of life were of great interest to the players on the team. Before they were going to trust me, they wanted to see whether my life was worthy of respect. Though they didn't demand perfection of me, who I was and how I conducted my life up until that moment were very important to them. They were interested in the dynamic between me and my own kids, all of whom were older than them, my marriage, and even my pets. I realized that to gain their respect I would have to open myself up some and let them look inside.

While we as coaches certainly have the right to our privacy and to maintain a life apart from our coaching responsibilities, know that our teams will gather information about our lives and will make their own assessment. If our lives reflect a lack of core values and are characterized by drama and a lack of class, the respect we seek will be difficult to secure. Knowing that we can coach is not enough; they want to know who we are.

Negativity is yet another way to chip away at the respect we seek from our players. We may not even be aware of the negative statements and declarations we make, but a negative spirit can be detrimental to everyone involved. A pessimistic attitude would never do for a general leading troops to battle, yet coaches routinely make statements laden with a negative outlook. I know of a Division I program where the players kept a notebook hidden in the dugout. On that notepad the players wrote down every negative, pessimistic statement that came out of their head coach's mouth. The book was quite thick, full of expressions of doubt from the lips of their leader.

Players respect us as coaches for reasons we are sometimes not even aware of. My head coach ended every practice with the reading of the "verse of the day." This daily Bible verse was simply read without explanation or elaboration to wrap up our time together with the team at practice. This was not a time of preaching, just an expression of her faith meant to pass on a few words of wisdom every day. The team always seemed to listen to the words and take them in stride without a response or reaction.

One year we had a player on the team who I thought may have been offended by the words of the Bible based on what I knew of her life. She was an engaging and hard-working individual, and I always wondered

Chapter 7. Respect Is Everything

what she thought of these verses coming to her every practice day. One time, in fact the only time, the head coach forgot to read the Bible verse. As Coach dismissed the team, the team arose and began to shuffle out of the dugout. This player suddenly spoke up, saying in a loud voice, "What about the Bible verse?" The tradition the head coach maintained of reading a daily verse was something this player respected, even if her life was often times not in accord with the words. She wanted to hear the verse that day. Her reminding Coach of her omission was a sign of respect. The admirable and positive things we do in our daily lives are often sources of respect from our team. If I learned nothing else that day, I learned that our players are watching us, looking for reasons to respect us or to lose that respect.

Jacksonville State University Head Coach Jana McGinnis speaks of the foundational role respect has had in her 26 seasons at JSU. With nearly 900 wins and seven post-season NCAA appearances to her credit, she speaks as one of the most respected coaches in Division I:

> It may be because of the way my parents raised me, but I have always believed that in life, respect is everything. In athletics, it may not really be everything, but respect is essential! This means that it is absolutely needed in order to have a successful program. There are a few things that are essential for a program to be successful, but without respect there can be no success. As a coach, I must show respect to my players, my authority, my environment and those whom I encounter daily. In return, I expect my players to do the same. Each player must also respect the game.

These are extremely strong words about respect from a proven and highly respected coaching veteran. Coach McGinnis couldn't make it any plainer. She uses words like "essential," "absolutely needed," and "success." Our daily goal must be to earn and retain the respect of our players. Coach McGinnis emphasizes giving respect to her players as well, leading by her example. By doing so she creates an environment where respect is a key component of the DNA of her highly successful program.

Another highly successful long-term head coach with a successful tenure of twenty seasons at the University of North Georgia, Mike Davenport emphasizes respect for the program and for the players and coaches who went before. Rather than focusing primarily on respect for himself, Coach Davenport directs his players' attention on the UNG winning tradition and their own part in the legacy handed down from player to player:

Coaching Women's Softball

In our program we feel it is important to pay tribute to our past so our players, coaches, and even our fans have an opportunity to celebrate those relationships that were built every season. There is no greater learning opportunity than to listen to those who have walked in your shoes before and want nothing more than to see you succeed while wearing the same jersey that they may have worn years before.

A constant in our program is this—"Honor / Respect Those Who Played the Game Before You."

You will see this quote on the back of our number 42 Jackie Robinson practice t-shirt each season as well as on the back on our bullpens at the field. It is important for our current players, coaches, fans to play the game, teach the game, and cheer for the game in a manner that honors those who made this game possible for us to play it each day and that is a great responsibility and privilege to do so.

What happens when a player loses respect for her coach? It is difficult for a player to move forward from that place. When presented with the statement: "If I lost respect for my coach, it would be harder to perform at my best for him/her" 82 percent marked "True." If we decide to lie, to name call, to play favorites, to lose our temper, to act improperly towards a player, we do so at a great cost. The respect we worked hard to earn can be gone in a moment. Players have long memories and are not obligated to overlook or forgive inappropriate or uncontrolled behavior. Without the foundation of respect, the house we are trying to build will not stand.

A standout infielder speaks of another deathblow to respect: favoritism. It takes very little for our players to conclude that we prefer some players over others. This perception, whether true or not, can infect your team with distrust and accusations that we carry our favoritism onto the field. An outstanding infielder makes this point: "I lost respect for a coach twice in my life. The first time was simple. Coaches are not friends. Coaches are coaches. This doesn't mean you can't be 'friendly' with your coach. This means that when other players are spending time with the coach away from the field, offices, or team activities, it automatically puts tension on the entire team."

Avoiding the appearance of favoritism may mean limiting access to certain players who have the tendency to want to hang out with us an inordinate amount of time. Being seen with a few of the same players starts the fires of jealousy and the perception of favoritism. We can be there for our players whenever they need us without spending a great deal more time with some as opposed to others.

Chapter 7. Respect Is Everything

The perception that we favor one player over another is one we must go to great lengths to dispel. Once a player feels that we have determined that another is more valued than her, it is difficult for her to believe that we believe otherwise.

I found that I had to be extremely careful with this issue when it came to my pitchers. I had three pitchers in almost consecutive recruiting classes whom I had taught since they were young. Having a previous close relationship with all three, I had to be careful not to signal that I valued my relationship with one over the other. Additionally, I had many other pitchers through the years whom I did not have as prior students. These players were watching carefully to see whether I was going to treat them the same as those I had known for years.

Factual statements that implied that one was better than the other or even actions that expressed that thought (like who is in the #1 position and pitching the first game of a series or double hitter) can offend. But the cold fact is that typically one is better than the others, and this is a part of life they must come to accept. How we handle that disparity is key. We make that decision based solely on merit, without a hint of anything that could be misconstrued as favoritism.

Another source of favoritism accusations stem from texts and social media interaction with certain players. Even though our texts may be mundane and perfectly proper, when some players receive information that others do not, it sets you up for accusations of favoritism. If you comment on one player's Facebook or Instagram page, the rest will question, "Why hers and not mine?" This can be all it takes for jealousy to take root and fingers to point at us for playing favorites.

This infielder continues on to relate her experience of losing total respect for her coach because of the coach's inability to stand up to players who needed it: "We had a freshmen class come in that respected nothing, not even the coach. And worst of all, the coach really didn't even know how to stand up to them. This freshmen class was the first recruiting class that this coach had brought on campus. A lack of respect was single handedly the entire reason this team fell apart. When the underclassmen wouldn't (not couldn't) respect the upperclassmen or the coach, I one hundred percent lost respect for the coach as a leader."

We cannot expect our players to follow our leadership if we demonstrate weakness when challenged. In this case the player considered her coach weak because she was passive, allowing these freshman to trample on her because she took the easy way. This upperclassman watched as a disrespectful freshman class undid the hard work they had put into building a special program. Expecting their coach, their leader, to step up, they instead saw her hide from her responsibilities.

Although we as coaches expect respect from them, we must give our players the respect they deserve. Respecting others is the key to gaining their respect in every arena, yet we as coaches sometimes neglect this maxim. As a rookie police officer in Miami in the 1970s, my veteran training officer gave me valuable advice that stuck with me. He told me, "You can't fight with every person you come into contact on the street. What you want is cooperation, and you get cooperation by giving respect to people." That advice applies to coaching as well.

An All-American first baseman tells of how she lost respect for a coach who showed her none:

> I lost respect for a coach when he didn't respect me. I know that respect is earned, and I work hard for something like that. But I had a coach that would constantly tear me down even when it had nothing to do with my sport. He would rag on me about my weight all of the time and tell me he didn't think I was good enough to play defense. I felt like nothing I did was good enough. I would hit 3 home runs in one game and he would try to fix my swing at practice [because] what I was doing wasn't working good enough. It was like no matter what I did, it was never enough. So that is why I lost respect for my coach. He never respected me or made me feel like I deserved to be on the field. I believe a coach has to respect their athletes to get full respect back, and when they don't work to show them they do respect them, then it will cause athletes to lose respect for them and make it hard to believe or buy in to what a coach is saying or asking of you.

When we as coaches think we can move a program forward without making respect a priority, we are doomed to failure because we have failed to recognize it as an absolute essential. Jacksonville State University Coach Jana McGinnis explains the role of respect in a successful program: "When building any foundation, there must be cornerstones. The cornerstones are what keeps a foundation at its maximum strength and enables you to continue to build on the foundation. Through all my years as a college softball coach, I have always believed that for our program to be strong and grow, it must be built with respect as a cornerstone."

Coach McGinnis has identified this trait as a "must have" when she evaluates potential recruits. Her experience tells her that the player whose demeanor shows little respect for herself and the image she

Chapter 7. Respect Is Everything

projects will have difficulty respecting coaches: "A person who respects themselves will have higher standards and expectations for themselves than what others place on them. If a person does not respect themselves, it will be very hard for them to have respect for coaches, teammates, standards of the program, and the game."

When I was recruiting a player, I spent much of my time observing her behavior off the field. What was the dynamic with her coach in the dugout? How did she react when the coach corrected her? Perhaps most important was how she interacted with her parents, and them with her. Was she disrespectful, dismissive, or even verbally abusive to them after a game? I felt that if this young lady didn't grasp the concept of respect for authority, we would never be able to instill in her the respect for us we required as coaches. I witnessed players yell at parents. I saw them turn and walk away while parents were trying to speak to them. I saw players argue with their coaches. I observed some put on a show of rebellion through body language and facial expressions when corrected. Perhaps because some of these young athletes have been pedestalized for so long, they have developed an entitled, disrespectful attitude. Whatever the reason, if we want to preserve a program where there is respect between coaches and players, we should proceed with caution when we see the flashing yellow lights surrounding a disrespectful potential recruit.

To our players, our episodes of rage, verbal abuse, dishonesty, favoritism, and cowardice are simply indicators of who we are as people. An All-Conference pitcher summarizes the issue from her perspective: "Many coaches lack the qualities to reach their players." To the extent that we lack the qualities our players are looking for, we will continue to fail to garner their respect.

Jacksonville State University Head Coach McGinnis sums up the importance of a coach having the respect of the team and how that respect can trump many issues: "Respect will take care of a lot of issues that arise as a coach."

Chapter 8

Know the Game

Female athletes, especially at the high school and college levels, generally know the game they have played their whole life. If we don't really know what we are doing as coaches, they will know it in no time. We can follow every suggestion in this book and fail miserably if we are incompetent. We must take every opportunity to evolve as a coach, to know what we are doing. We can't let laziness or pride get in our way. We must be competent. We must learn and then learn some more.

It is our responsibility to not only develop the relational skills necessary for the task; we must be skilled in the technical dimension of coaching as well. We must possess both. We won't make an impact on their lives without both ... and we won't win either.

If we want to be a great coaches, we must start with being great learners. We must possess a passion to learn more about the game. We have chosen to coach fastpitch softball as our profession. We shortchange ourselves when we refuse to coach to our full potential, a potential that can be limited by our technical incompetency. Yet this is one dimension that can be changed in the time it takes to make a commitment to get better. We can challenge ourselves to become a more knowledgeable coach, to overcome our own laziness and complacency. Our players are watching to see whether we are growing in knowledge, or if we remain the same year after year.

Perennial power programs remain that way because of good coaching. Coaches that learn and evolve win. They regularly outcoach opponents. They prepare their players better and know how to extract the best from them. While many coaches bemoan the hindrances they face where they coach, the growing coaches, the smart ones, are finding ways to win on the field in spite of things like facilities, location, or climate. They overcome not only by knowing how to connect with, lead, and love their players. They also know the game and are seeing to it that they know it better every year.

Chapter 8. Know the Game

Our players are watching us in games and in practice to see what we know. Do we just repackage the same body of knowledge each year, never progressing in our practice routine or game savvy? We don't have to pile onto the latest hitting or defense drills video. We simply must be learning more, becoming more efficient in practice and more skilled in games.

If we want characterize woman's softball coaching as a profession, we must conform to the demands that qualify it as such. No doctor, teacher, attorney, or accountant would consider relying on the knowledge base they possessed their first day at work. They build upon their education. They learn, developing their skills as a professional. They progress, becoming better with time because they never stop learning. So it must be with us as coaches. This is our profession, one where those who commit to develop and increase their knowledge base will bypass the lazy and ignorant among us.

I don't claim to possess a great level of softball knowledge, but I have to say that while watching my daughter play college softball, I was regularly amazed at the game decisions made by some of her opponent's coaches. Though these were Division I programs, there were obvious gaps in these coaches' knowledge of the game. Were they capable of learning? Of course they were. I suppose they were just too lazy to develop as a professional coach, satisfied to be drinking milk while the smart coaches were eating solid food.

When I began coaching in college as a second career, I saw more of the same. I saw coaches who refused to research opponents, would not contact other coaches for game notes, and went into games without benefit of hitting or pitching charts from past games. This was simply ignorance and laziness masquerading as confidence. Preferring to react to the game as it unfolded rather than having a plan going in, the coach limited the success of the team. This coach was working off of ego rather than intelligence.

Coming from a previous career in federal law enforcement, I was used to a work environment where training and individual development was mandatory. Keeping up with new laws and court decisions, firearms training, and tactical and self defense practice forced you to become safer, better, and smarter. Having no such structure in coaching to rely upon, it is incumbent on us to expose ourselves to great coaches and ideas to simply get better. We must avail ourselves to new information and better ways to function as a leader and a coach.

Coaching Women's Softball

Our players observe and take note of our coaching weak spots, our predictable, repeated decisions whenever a particular situation arises during a game. They also catalog the success or failure of our decisions. If we cling to pet strategies that are not beneficial to winning overall, our players know it and comment to one another when our strategy fails. We have to be willing to take a fresh look at the game strategy we have always used. It may have weak spots that we need to change. Being open about it, we must let our players know we are all about winning and are willing to change our own favorite strategies if it helps the team. Putting our egos aside, we must learn, change, and evolve.

As a pitching coach, I had subscribed to a pitching strategy over the years of having the starter go as many innings as possible and pulling them in favor of a reliever only when they got into trouble or began to lose their effectiveness. This plan seemed to work out well, so I may have developed a blind spot toward changing my mind on the matter. One year my starting pitchers both developed the tendency to pitch wonderfully for five innings or so, and in the sixth suddenly lose their effectiveness. By the time this developed, runs were scored or at least opposing runners were on base threatening to score. Of course, at that point the starter would be pulled in favor of a reliever, but it was often too late, and the game was already effectively lost.

One of the relievers, a highly intelligent and analytical person, presented me with a solution. She suggested that we try having the starters go five innings, then replace them in the sixth regardless of how well they might be doing. At first, I resisted this great idea but eventually adopted this player's suggestion. At least for the short term, this was a needed change. It put an end to the dreaded sixth inning pitching troubles. The starters didn't like it one bit, but it actually enabled them to take a break from the sixth inning jinx and focus on pitching well for five innings. In the end, the relief pitcher was credited with a great idea, I learned that I could change my long-held strategies, and the team won more games.

Our players want and deserve coaches who are innovative and progressive. Not that we should be different just for difference's sake, but for the thinker there are always new ideas to embrace. Starting out as a college pitching coach, for the first time I had my pitchers full-time, year-round rather than for an hour a week at a pitching lesson, or the limited time a travel or high school team allowed. Much more so than

Chapter 8. Know the Game

in coaching travel ball or high school, I could dictate how much they pitched in their bullpen sessions and how much they rested. I already knew based on documented fastpitch studies that the underhand motion was at least as destructive as overhand baseball pitching. This evidence ran counter to conventional wisdom in softball that asserts that the underhand motion is harmless and pitchers from the age of ten can pitch multiple games per day without risk of injury. I knew from watching my daughter's college career that she was made to throw way too much during the season, and there really was no systematic plan behind her practice routine. The well-established baseball pitching wisdom of rest days, light days, and recovery days were not generally embraced in the college softball world. I decided that my pitchers were going to be in a program that included rest days after pitching games, bull pens that peaked in intensity midweek, and very light days on the day before games. There was also careful planning of their weight training and conditioning in proximity to game days. This plan would be accepted as normal in the baseball world but subjected me to criticism from coaches who sincerely felt that more was always better. The results spoke for themselves as our pitchers led the conference in most measurements year in and year out. My pitchers appreciated my determination to put them in the best possible position to succeed. They appreciated that I was being a thinker, not simply a sheep doing what everyone else did.

As coaches, we can tend to become followers instead of leaders when it comes to the latest coaching fad. Often new angles on understanding technical aspects of the game come upon the scene. New gurus emerge and new drills are championed on YouTube, videos promising instant success. Rather than taking time and brainpower to evaluate a new program, we often endorse it and foist it upon our team. This can be a good thing if these new theories are properly screened and considered. But when we go to the latest, greatest fad on a regular basis, our players see a coach with no center and no ideas of his own. The particular new idea might be great for certain athletes or certain teams but not for others. Be a thinker, always looking for real paths to improvement. Think on weaknesses of individual players and bring them well thought out solutions and drills that address that player.

UAB Head Coach Joe Guthrie shared a situation where coaching skill and game knowledge resulted in a huge improvement in performance:

Coaching Women's Softball

One of the primary tenets in my experience coaching softball has always been building confidence through competence. The ability to perform this task directly relates to a coach's knowledge of the game, but more importantly, being able to know when and how to impart that knowledge to their athlete. I believe this information is critical especially coaching the modern athlete.

For example, several years ago, while the Head Softball Coach at Marion Military Institute, I ran into a problem with one of our primary base stealing threats. This player opened the season getting thrown out attempting to steal second base multiple times. The previous year, she had rarely been thrown out at all. She and I had a joint meeting to determine why she was being thrown out stealing.

Through study of film of practice, we determined that she exhibited a false step in her steal break to second base. Upon realizing this mistake, I concluded that it was best to give her a metric that would allow her to eliminate the false step. If we eliminated the false step (which was why she was being thrown out), she would steal bases. Thus, I told her that any stolen base attempt without her exhibiting a false step would be marked down and praised as a success. I did not care whether she was out or safe. She eventually stole more bases, but more importantly she achieved this goal by following a process allowing her to eliminate any fear of simply being thrown out. She focused on simply eliminating the false step. We came to this conclusion by knowing what we were looking for and by setting the athlete up for giving the athlete a "process oriented" metric. Without knowing the game, I do not believe she would have trusted me or made the proper adjustment for success.

Coach Guthrie not only used his extensive knowledge of the game down to knowing the proper footwork to initiate a successful steal, he coupled it with a workable remedy: a remedy his athlete bought in to, and one that worked. Seeing this level of competency can garner respect from the entire team, creating an open door for learning and correction.

Female athletes at the college level have normally spent many years under the tutelage of a club team coach as well as high school coaches. Though we would be hesitant to admit it, many of these coaches are extremely competent, in many cases more experienced and knowledgeable that we are as college coaches. Additionally, many of our players had private skill coaches who again may have impressive backgrounds and knowledge bases. Like it or not, these are the coaches our players are comparing us to. Rather than downplaying the status of a club or

Chapter 8. Know the Game

high school team coach, we need to up our game and earn our players' respect just as these past coaches did.

A former Division I pitcher shared her frustrations with dealing with what she considered an incompetent college coach:

> A coach who does not know the game is a poor leader. From experience, this type of coach puts major stress on the players. For me specifically, I always had the desire to have a coachable reputation, but with a coach with lack of game knowledge, he and she not only hindered the team's ability to succeed with poor coaching decisions, but also severely frustrated all of us. This frustration turned to disrespect from the team. No team can succeed if there is not consistent, strong leadership. A coach with poor game knowledge will be aware of it. From experience, they second-guess and become frustrated with themselves. They quickly become emotional roller coasters, and can quickly take that frustration out on players, in turn, derailing their own program.

This pitcher describes a scenario where the players know more about the game than the coach. The players do not want to be in this position any more than a child wants to be driving a car. Our players don't want to drive; they want to play. Under a knowledgeable coach, they can relax and focus on their game, free from the anxiety an uninformed, insecure coach can bring.

A lack of technical competency is impossible to keep hidden. Games hinge on decisions, good and bad. William Peace Head Coach Charlie Dobbins sets out the importance of decisions based on solid knowledge: "Leaders, and in most cases coaches live and die by decision making. As the leader and implementer of the strategy, strive to improve your skills to put you in a better position to lead. You also set an example for others to improve their game."

Coaches who know their stuff command a certain measure of respect based on that alone. We once brought in a hitting coach to work with our hitters in the fall. As I introduced the coach, Francisco Matos, a minor league hitting coach in the Texas Rangers organization and a former major league baseball player, our players took notice, but I could tell that they were still withholding judgment. Once Coach Matos began to speak, to talk hitting, a hush came over the group. His knowledge was so deep, his insight so great, that the players were mesmerized by him. There was no quiet chatting, whispering, or horsing around as he taught hitting theory and technique. I couldn't get enough myself.

On the other hand, incompetency invites distrust and disrespect, as expressed by a former All-Conference pitcher: "Playing for a coach that doesn't know the game is one of the quickest ways to lose the respect of the team. The team will catch on and end up questioning every decision the coach makes from there on out. It is extremely difficult to execute a game plan when the team is not on board. It hinders your ability to play all out. From a pitching perspective, when I am questioning the pitch that has been called, I do not throw it with conviction because I am worried about it being the right call."

Birmingham Southern College Coach Kimball Cassady recalls her days as a player when playing for a coach who knew the game, yet couldn't relay that knowledge to her players: "I've been pretty blessed in my playing career to have had some really good coaches, but I have played for a few coaches that even though they knew the game, they didn't really know how to teach the game. Their communication was extremely bad, which made it look like they didn't know the game, but in actuality they really did. They just couldn't figure out how to communicate with the players."

Great coaches not only know what they are doing, they are all about providing the rationale for what is being taught. A former Big 12 pitcher speaks of the value of having a coach, including a strength coach, explain the why behind the what: "Our strength and conditioning coach was so down to earth and really explained how and why we would do all the extra training/running/lifting we would do. We even just played volleyball, basketball or different games to train instead of just running for conditioning. He made it fun for us."

Having to stand by in silence and watch an incompetent coach undermine the team's success can be a frustrating experience for a player. An All-Region pitcher describes what it's like to watch a coach make mistakes based on ignorance: "Playing for a coach that did not know the game was awful because you would see them doing something and making a call that was awful for the team, but there was no way to tell your coach respectfully or nicely that you think they're making the wrong call. You basically feel helpless because you are watching something that shouldn't be happening happen, and there is nothing you can do about it."

A coach who doesn't know the game does more than cause the team to fail in game situations. This same pitcher describes what happens when individual players receive poor instruction from their coach: "It is also hard because you're not getting the right critique

Chapter 8. Know the Game

or meaningful feedback to assist your game. You could potentially be getting wrong feedback that they expect you to follow. This makes it especially difficult when you know that the advice you are getting is wrong."

An outstanding second baseman questions whether an incompetent coach is a coach at all: "When a coach doesn't 'know' the game, or what I refer to as the mental component of on-field play, decision making is cloudy at best. A lack of understanding of situational hitting, field positions, or more can lead to so many wrong paths. Development of an understanding of the game has to happen prior to leading others on the field. It seems to be the basic building block of becoming a coach."

An All-Region outfielder tells of the negative impact incompetent coaching has on both the individual and on the team:

> An incompetent coach is easily the most frustrating thing in the world to me. Having someone coach you and break down the minuscule details (that should be making athletes better), and said coach not understanding the game itself, is horrifying. Specifically in softball, making coaching mistakes can cause a momentum shift that cannot be overcome. Coaches should be involved in the momentum in the dugout, on the bench, or around the field. They should know the X's and O's situationally in full and understand how easy it is to slip. Overall, knowledge of the game itself is vital to any success.

An All-Conference pitcher speaks of how playing for a coach who does not know the game puts pressure on players to manage their own part of the game: "Playing for a coach that did not know the game made me feel that I had to run the game myself. Having a coach run the game would have made my job a lot easier as a pitcher. Trusting in their knowledge and strategy would have allowed me to concentrate on my job."

Closely related to the coach who lacks knowledge of the game is the one who insists that everyone subscribe to his or her way of doing things. While there are certainly non-negotiables, a good coach knows the difference between a preference and an absolute. An All-Conference pitcher and hitter describes what it was like to be forced to adopt a coach's preference:

> I have been fortunate enough in my lifetime to have coaches that were consistent and knowledgeable in the sports that I played, especially

softball. In my lifetime, I have played for coaches that are in the Hall of Fame and ones that are labeled as the best in their league. With their time and effort with me, I have been able to obtain many of awards such as Conference Pitcher of the Year, First-Team All Conference on numerous occasions, and so on.

    I wouldn't necessarily say that I have played for a coach that didn't know the game, but more so a coach that believed that there was only one way to hit a softball. At the college level, you would think that coaches like this didn't exist, but they do. This coach shunned me as a hitter; she believed that since I was a pitcher, I was incapable of hitting. (I snickered at this too and then proceeded to hit 8 out of 10 out in live that day.) At first I allowed her opinion to affect the way I played. I had to realize that her beliefs were far different from mine (or how I was taught). Once I made that realization and put it into action by not letting it bother me, the coach noticed and shunned me. I saw this same thing happening with other great hitters on the team as well. I also saw it take a toll on other teammates ... they lost confidence, couldn't discover their worth as a player, and some even quit the sport.

    With coaches that may not be the best or even lack the knowledge, the player has to have enough discipline and will-power to get past the ignorance and just play the sport they love. At the college level, you (as a player) cannot let anyone take away from your God-given talents. Overcome because that is what GREAT players do.

As coaches we need to be aware of the very human tendency to believe that our way is the only way. As a pitching coach, I had to constantly remind myself that there are many styles within fastpitch pitching, different body types with different mechanical capabilities. I found the most helpful thing for me was to boil down pitching to four essentials. I would present these non-negotiables to my students and pitchers on our team as the four legs of a table. Without any one of the supporting legs, the table collapses under its own weight. There was room for variety in the rest of the pitching motion, and that was room I had to give my pitchers. I had to be open to suggestion, as long as the pitcher's preference didn't involve the four legs, and as long as what she was doing worked. Knowing that I was not there to "change" them or create a clone, they could relax and work on getting better. There was simply no good reason to unnecessarily push them out of their comfort zone just to satisfy me. I had to ask myself what my objective was. Am I here to make this athlete into the best pitcher she could possibly be or is it to stamp out yet another pitcher who pitches exactly how I prefer?

Chapter 8. Know the Game

Are we properly prepared for games? Our players depend on us to research our opponents and to prepare the team accordingly. If we aren't doing our due diligence in this area, the players will take note, as this pitcher explains: "Experience and knowledge of the game are the most important characteristics of a successful leader. My coach immersed herself in statistical analysis and made it a priority to know her opponents better than she knew herself. In addition, the quality of practices also amplified my respect for this coach. Clear communication and having an itinerary posted beforehand set the tone for what to expect. This resulted in high quality and efficient practices."

Wisconsin Associate Head Coach Danielle Zymkowitz tells of how her love for learning the game as a player has continued on now that she is in the coaching role:

> I loved winning. I loved asking my coaches what they were seeing on the other side of the lines. I loved studying the X's and O's of the game. This quest for learning and knowledge of the game helped me start to fall in love with leading my teammates in a different way than what I was used to. I started to see the game as a coach. One of the most important things I learned through playing in the NPF was there is not one way to play this game. At the beginning of every season with the Bandits, I would try to hit with a different rookie every day. I would ask them what their hitting philosophies were at the programs they played in? Their favorite drills? How they approached hitting a certain pitch? What their pre-pitch routine was? How they liked to set up certain hitters? The list of questions goes on and on. I also have had teammates from Japan, Australia, Mexico and played against Canadians and Chinese. They play the game different than us Americans. Now as a coach, nothing has changed. I love learning what the best of the best does; who doesn't? It's hard as a coach to put yourself out there and tell your players that you do not have all the answers. In my case, I am not ashamed of being a lifelong learner, and I believe our players respect me for that. If they have a question that I do not know the answer to, I will reach out to my mentors to try and find an answer for them. By setting the example, I expect them to also have that same mentality. We study the game at University of Wisconsin. We watched games together from the WCWS to learn and see what the best in our sport do, so hopefully one day we will be there.

Coach Zymkowitz (Coach "Z" as she is known) is a self-described "lifelong learner," a designation shared by all great softball coaches. Instead of resting on her impressive pedigree as a two-time All-

Coaching Women's Softball

American and veteran NPF player, she continues to learn from others. In doing so, she garners the upmost respect from her players.

An encounter I had with a Division I coach showed me just how resistant to improvement even a longtime coach can be. I had retired from my college coaching job in Alabama to move to Texas to help out with grandkids. Having some time on my hands, I decided to offer my services as a volunteer pitching coach to a college in my area. I did my homework and knew that the team had suffered consecutive losing seasons, and their pitching numbers were horrific. I also knew that the young assistant coach handling the pitchers had many other duties and had no background as a pitcher or as a pitching coach.

Since I had tried to contact the head coach via email and got no response, I decided to pay her an in-person visit. As I entered the open door to the head coach's office, both she and her assistant were seated. The head coach never looked at me directly as I introduced myself. No response. Neither coach looked up or introduced themselves. I offered to volunteer if they needed pitching expertise, presenting my pitching coach credentials for her consideration. Without bragging, I let her know what I had accomplished along with my pitchers in terms of wins and relevant statistics. I offered to provide references including coaches of teams she had played against. Without even speaking a word or making eye contact she dismissed me, informing me that they had it covered. Now, I understand that she was under no obligation to consider adding a volunteer coach, but her arrogance didn't match up with her program, especially with her pitching stats. She needed help and had an opportunity to get help (for free!) but was satisfied to continue on doing the same things that produced failure in the past. I have to imagine that the pitchers on that team would have welcomed a new set of eyes to help them win. Their coaches' prideful attitude robbed them of that opportunity. Such is the power of arrogance and insecurity.

This attitude that a coach already has enough knowledge is something I sometimes saw when instructing pitching clinics. These clinics would be held on college campuses and typically included players from early teens through high school. When speaking to the group about pitching mechanics, training, strategy, etc., I would invite these players' coaches (who were often also their dads) who were often present in the stands to come onto the field and listen in.

What troubled me is that typically only half of these youth coaches took advantage of the offer. My hope was that these coaches would widen their knowledge base and be there to reinforce the coaching

Chapter 8. Know the Game

points I was imparting to the young pitchers. This attitude that a coach, whether at the youth level or in Division I, already has enough knowledge of the game is driven by pride and laziness. A good coach takes every opportunity to learn. Without being a learner, we stagnate and settle.

Our players depend upon us to get better. Over 99 percent of players surveyed marked "True" to the statement: "It is very important to me that my coach's knowledge of the game is at a high level." We expect them to get better, and they expect the same from us.

Texas Lutheran Head Coach Wade Wilson believes that it is not only coaches who need to have a strong knowledge of the game, but players should excel in that area as well. He specifically recruits players whose game knowledge rises above the rest. It takes a coach who is confident in his or her own understanding of softball to seek out such players. These players are drawn to college programs run by sharp coaches, and they are able to detect those who are weak in this area. The lazy or unmotivated coach, the one whose knowledge of the sport is suspect, often loses out on recruiting softball smart players because the players are looking for something better in a coach. Coach Wilson explains:

> As a college coach we are always trying to find and recruit athletes that stick out. When you come across kids that "know the game" or have a high softball IQ they usually stand out like a ship in a pond. These kids are, however, getting harder to find. I once had a coach tell me that if you can get five kids that want to win as bad as you do, you will have a championship team. I agree totally with this statement. To add to that, if you can find five kids that know the game, that is another recipe for a championship team. We are typically a very aggressive offensive team. There is more to that than just speed, although speed is the key component. We spend a bunch of time on situations that can create havoc for the defense. You have kids that know exactly what we are doing and trying to accomplish; for the others, you have to spend time working on the concept daily. What a thrill as a coach when you see the light turn on for those kids.

Our players are looking for a coach who is softball smart ... and getting smarter every year. They want a coach who has an answer for the various situations that present themselves in the course of a softball game. They want someone who can diagnose and remedy the technical and mechanical issues that are holding them back. The coach they seek is not perfect and makes their share of mistakes on the field. They just want a smart coach who is knowledgeable about softball, a growing coach who is not afraid to look at things from a new angle. In short, they want someone who knows what they are doing.

Christopher Newport Head Coach Keith Parr sums up the necessity to keep learning. With over 500 wins to his credit, he speaks as one of the winningest coaches in Division III:

> Being knowledgeable about the game is an integral part of finding success as a coach. Just like in life, one should never stop learning and trying to improve. This is an important concept to both coach and player. As a coach, it is critical that you continue to be a student of the game and continue to evolve for your team and players. The subsequent challenge is finding a way to convey that information to your players that they can easily comprehend and put into practice. Next steps involve creating opportunities for the players to get better faster while using this knowledge to take their game to the next level. That is the challenge and goal of each coach!

Chapter 9

A Coach's Agenda

I wonder how many of us have actually articulated what it is we are trying to accomplish as coaches besides winning games. We have seen that winning games and loving our players are not mutually exclusive. Indeed, tending to the emotional and personal needs of our players enhances our winning percentage. As we become intentional about what we hope to accomplish with our coaching careers in terms of impacting lives, our overall strategy comes into focus.

I offer a suggested list of goals, a statement of intentions we can strive to adhere to and to fulfill. Though we will fall short of perfection, when we remain committed to the principles, we become better mentors, better examples, and better coaches.

1. Know Softball

Without this component we lack the foundation of respect to accomplish much of anything, whether on the field or in the lives of players. Notice how NPF Chicago Bandit Jenna Lilley relates the technical coaching ability of Jimmy Kolaitis with the mentoring he does:

> On top of all this, yes, he is also an incredible coach and hitting guru. Coach K flat out knows his stuff, and more importantly, he was a great teacher who was always willing to keep learning himself. He would always be there for us to get in extra work whenever we wanted. Whether you were in the starting nine or the last one off the bench, Coach would be there for you to get better, and you could really feel that in the way he interacted with you during those extra sessions. Most of the time they would turn into life talks. Sure, we got in great work, but we also had a great time doing it.

All of the love we give and connections we make will fall flat unless our technical knowledge is strong ... and growing. Make the commitment to be better, more knowledgeable and more engaged with the fine techniques and advanced game strategies. With a broader knowledge of drills and practice routines, we show our players that we are working hard to get them better, rather than rolling out the same tired practice routine. It will take some digging and some research, but we must be smart about training, drilling, and actually coaching in game situations.

As we fight to overcome our own resistance to change, we become free thinkers, always looking to be a better coach. Pushing our natural laziness aside, we move forward as the competent coach we must be.

UAB Head Coach Joe Guthrie makes the connection between teaching the game and knowing it yourself: "One of the primary tenants [sic] in my experience coaching softball has always been building confidence through competence. The ability to perform this task directly relates to a coach's knowledge of the game...."

If our knowledge base is too shallow, we have nothing to give to elevate the skill level of our players. William Peace Head Coach Charlie Dobbins explains that unless we are learners, improving our coaching skills, we shouldn't expect our players to improve: "Leaders, and in most cases coaches, live and die by decision making. As the leader and implementer of the strategy, strive to improve your skills to put you in a better position to lead. You also set an example for others to improve their game."

When our level of competency is less than it should be, we are unable to succeed in any dimension of coaching our team. Our ability to improve our players in individual sessions will be severely limited. Our practices may be long and grueling, but unless we are smart about what we implement and repeat during that time, we are accomplishing little. Consistently bad game coaching on our part will lose games, and everyone will notice.

As much as the techniques, mechanics, and strategies of softball remain the same, the methods we use continue to evolve. Video software enhances our ability to improve hitting. Pitching drills that were the meat and potatoes of pitching development have now been discarded by coaches who keep their knowledge base up to date. The understanding of the role of the internal rotation of the arm and wrist has opened up new possibilities in velocity and spin. The pitching coach who is clinging to a 1990s understanding of pitching does a disservice to his pitchers and adds to the losses column. Whether in the area of pitching, hitting, base running, or defense, we need to be up to speed.

Chapter 9. A Coach's Agenda

Early in my career as an ATF Special Agent, I was assigned an undercover assignment where I was to form a relationship with a Mafia debt collector/enforcer, a profession commonly known as a "leg breaker." Though I had prior experience as a police officer, I had never worked undercover and knew virtually nothing about how to go about it, especially if things did not go as planned. I had to not only make a viable criminal case against this character, but more importantly, stay alive. I was confident about portraying myself as someone else to this man (in this case I played a hit man from Miami), but what about if at some point during the undercover operation (which lasted weeks), things suddenly went south. I went to two very skilled and experienced undercover agents and picked their brains. What if he accuses me of being the police? What if he shows up and has other thugs with him? What if he wants to change the meet location or wants to take me in the car with him? All of these situations and more were discussed with advice given by them and received by me. I gained the benefit of the combined experience of those two brave and streetwise special agents.

After meeting with the "leg breaker" for several weeks, it was agreed that he would show me the residence of a person he wanted killed. After receipt of half of the money he was to pay me, he would be arrested by my "cover team," a squad of agents who were electronically monitoring my conversation and surveilling my movements with the suspect in my car with me. Unfortunately, as is often the case, things did not go as planned. Unbeknownst to me, the cover team, including a surveillance aircraft, lost me as soon as I pulled out of the parking lot with the leg breaker in the passenger seat. As we talked about his desire for me to murder this person, the tape-recorded evidence was mounting against him. At about this time, I looked in horror as the microphone from a hidden tape recorder fell out of the headliner just behind the rearview mirror. The technician who installed the wire had failed to secure it properly behind the headliner ... so I had a dangling wire with a tiny microphone on the end hanging in front of the leg breaker's face. Though I couldn't have anticipated this disaster, the training I received from the experienced agents came back to me. I remained calm, even though I had a 6'8" 300-pound ex-con who hurts people for a living sitting next to me. He asked me what that wire was (add several expletives). I just shrugged, told him I had only borrowed the car, all the while silently reaching under my shirt for my Walther PPK pistol. After a moment, leg breaker saw that I was calm so he calmed down and accepted my explanation, implausible as it was.

We resumed our conversation where we left off, and he paid me the amount of money agreed upon and continued to incriminate himself in taped conversation. It was time to have the cover team pull me over and arrest both of us. As I gave the verbal signal over the "wire" to arrest, nothing happened. I put my arm out the window and signaled that it was game time, again nothing. I realized nobody was coming to help me, but that was acceptable because I had been taught that this happens at times and already had a plan to succeed. Pulling the car over suddenly, I told the leg breaker that I needed to be sick. He seemed confused by this. I opened my door and headed behind the car where I drew my gun, pointed it at him, and ordered him out of the car. He complied, and the cover team pulled up just as I was finishing cuffing his very large wrists.

The point is that being knowledgeable equals being prepared. And being prepared equals being successful. I could have gone on the undercover assignment without the wisdom and instruction of the two experienced special agents. After all, I had survived years as a cop in Miami, one of the most violent cities in America. But if I had, I may not have survived. We can't afford to just go with what we know. To succeed, to avoid disaster, learn and become a knowledgeable softball coach.

2. Make the Connection

This is an area where we may think we are doing pretty well as coaches, yet my research suggests this is not necessarily the case. Almost thirty percent of college softball players indicated that their coach had not made a strong effort to connect with them. Players who were interviewed stressed the necessity of a connection with their coach, not only for their emotional well-being, but for their success on the field. This desire for connection with us revolves around them being perceived as more than just an athlete. There are so many dimensions to the lives of these young women, aspects they want us to recognize and embrace. Time after time we hear the same refrain, that they want us to be interested in their personal lives. They want to see if we are willing to take the time to get to know them and to expend the emotional energy necessary to deepen that understanding. They want to be appreciated for more than their rise ball or base stealing ability, but unless we deepen our relationship with them, we won't really know them, much less appreciate them.

Agreeing that connection is important, even essential, is not

Chapter 9. A Coach's Agenda

enough. As Arizona State Assistant Coach Jimmy Kolaitis said, "By having a strategy in place, we pursue our athletes." That strategy may differ according to the athlete. As Coach Dorrance puts it, "Whatever the relationship is, it must be a relationship of their choosing. They will let you know what they need, or don't, and it is your job to respond."*

Connecting is one way that we can best mentor our athletes both during their brief time with us and into the future. The connection we make with a player enables us to remain as someone with a voice in her life, a respected resource for the daunting post-college years. The softball athlete deals not only with the transition from student to employee, she must adjust to a life without the sport that has consumed her since she was very young.

Like so many other coaches, I am privileged to have ongoing relationships with many former players, and it is a great source of blessing to me. I am honored that they seek my advice, or more frequently, just want me to listen to their plans or thoughts. None of this life mentoring would be taking place if the connection hadn't been made between us long ago on a softball field.

When our players know that we are interested in them as people and seek connection with them, the word spreads. As the team realizes that we sincerely care and want to be a part of their lives, this can go a long way towards them overlooking our many faults and shortcomings.

3. Earn Their Respect

It is possible to have a thorough knowledge of softball and be a great connector, and yet to fail as a coach. We have all seen it: the smart, charming, personable coach whom people are drawn to. It is often this type of coach who is ego-driven, perhaps even narcissistic in some cases, the type of coach who thinks players must respect him or her simply because of who they are.

This coach couldn't be more flawed in their thinking. Gaining and keeping the respect of our players is absolutely essential. Players base their respect level not on who we say we are or on who we think we are. They make their own assessment as to whether or not we are worthy of respect.

The respect of our players is a fragile commodity. Years of investment into our reputation can be lost in a moment of unwarranted anger,

---

*Dorrance, "Coaching Women."

verbal abuse, dishonesty, favoritism, improper relationships, or a lack of character in our personal lives.

The raging Bobby Knight style of coaching is a guaranteed respect killer and has no place in our sport. While sternness, intense correction when appropriate, or "tough love" can all serve to build the respect our players, straight up meanness, unbridled anger, and verbal degradation deal that same respect a deathblow. We must be mindful that what we say is being evaluated and catalogued by our players, and if we cross the line from needed correction to verbal bullying, there will be consequences in the respect department.

The competitiveness we all share as coaches must be balanced with the long view of what we are trying to accomplish beyond simply coaching. As William Peace Head Coach Charlie Dobbins reminds us, "Be cautious that 'the will to win' does not spill over into aggression." Knowing the tendency we all have to verbally take things too far, in the name of long-term respect, we must learn to bite our tongues at times.

Another area where respect can be easily lost is in how we deal with the selfish, toxic star player. The survey of college players revealed that 86 percent felt that selfish players negatively impacted the success of the team, yet 56 percent felt that their coach failed to control and deal with selfish star players. Our players are watching to see whether we have the character to stand up to these individuals. When we fail to do so, when we cave to them because of their athletic abilities, we lose respect we will not get back.

Eighty-two percent of the players surveyed agreed with the statement, "If I lost respect for my coach, it would be harder to perform at my best for him or her."

If we let that sink in, our only course of action is to seek to earn and keep the respect of our players, no matter what.

4. Love the Person, Then the Player

There is no more important mission for us as coaches than to love the players entrusted to us. To create a relationship characterized by genuine caring, sacrificial giving, and sincere concern is the most noble path we can possibly take. What good have we done if we develop our players in strictly athletic terms? It is our opportunity, our privilege to love these athletes not for stats they put up for us but for who they are as young women. As Oregon State Head Coach and four-time Olympian

Chapter 9. A Coach's Agenda

Laura Berg put it, "I feel it's essential for your players to know that you love them not only as softball players but as people too."

Loving our players as people comes down to time and effort. Those expenditures will not go unnoticed by our young people. Our sincerity will show through as we place our athletes above ourselves. There is no question that this is exactly what our players want: to be loved unconditionally. Yet only 75 percent of college softball players surveyed agreed with the statement, "My coach loves me unconditionally and has my back."

What level of love are our players looking for from us? The standard is high, to be sure. As an All-American shortstop said in describing her coach, "He cares for his girls as if they were his own." Another player, a member of a National Championship team, said of her coach, "As a father of three, he cared for each and every one of us as if we were his own." There it is. When we recruit a player, we accept responsibility to adopt them in a very real sense. A very special relationship begins, one in which we as coaches are the initiators, the doers when it comes to loving our players.

Loving our players is not optional if we seek to run a successful program on the field and to make a lasting impact on a life. As an NCAA Woman of the Year finalist said, "My head coach loved his players. There is no doubt about that. He told us he did multiple times, but his actions always spoke louder than his words."

5. Be the Leader

Leadership is the umbrella that covers all of the responsibilities of being a great coach to female athletes. A leader is competent, possessing knowledge of his or her sport. That competency, demonstrated day in and day out, in all situations and under every circumstance, is what compels our players to follow us into battle.

When we determine to act like a leader, other issues that detract from our program's success are minimized. The selfish toxic player who brings the team down by her actions and attitudes is neutralized by a strong leader who meets her head on. Disgruntled, negative players seeking to gain a following have a difficult time getting traction when the team is under our strong but benevolent leadership.

Our players are looking for a leader who is willing to have their backs beyond arguing a questionable play at the plate. We need to be that leader who is there when they need a strong presence in their corner. They want a coach who leads out of selflessness, not out of pride and ego. As an All-Conference pitcher explained, "Coaches I have had that have been great leaders have had no ego." How many of us would expect to be described in that way?

The determination to become a great leader can be a life-changing decision. When being that kind of a coach is our goal, we must be ready for a transformation. While competitiveness and passion are desired qualities, perhaps we need to frame those great attributes by being in control of our emotions. The same perceptive pitcher continues, "Another quality I've seen in great coaches that have been great leaders is the ability to maintain composure." As Coach Dobbins put it, "Your job is not to be too high or too low. In the heat of the moment it can be easy to lose sight of your vision by leading with the wrong one."

The transition from good coach to a great one will not be easy. Of the topics discussed in this book, the task of becoming the leader coach we desire to be may be the most difficult. The difficulty lies in the breadth of the role of "leader." This is a title we wear, one that we never take off. We are to be a strong, steady, perceptive, and knowledgeable leader in the locker room, in the bus, in our office, out in public, and on the field. There are no days off from this. That leader is who we are.

6. Know the Difference

We have explored areas of coaching female athletes that may have been underemphasized in the past. We have heard from forward-thinking college softball coaches who get it, who understand that these are not men we are coaching; they are women with a different set of preferences and expectations.

The understanding we gained from surveying and interviewing college softball players must be put to good use. The players have spoken; we know what they want from us as coaches. They cannot be coached, developed, or motivated in the same way as male athletes.

We saw how important a connection with her coach is to a female player, and that connection must extend well beyond her identity as an athlete. She must be more than simply an asset on our team. Connecting for a male is simply not a priority, and while a good relationship with his coach is a bonus, the male athlete can operate at full capacity as long as he is given the opportunity to play. If you have developed your coaching

Chapter 9. A Coach's Agenda

style based on coaching males, or from being an athlete yourself under a coach that operates under the male model, know that the level of connection under that system is inadequate when it comes to coaching females.

Although many coaches have advocated insisting on team love, we saw that this is not a possibility on most female softball teams. Female athletes will unite under competitiveness and the need to respect each other as players, but for most, team love is not a viable goal. On the other hand, famous coaches of male teams have stressed this love between all teammates with great results. The Detroit Pistons from the 1980s come to mind. While it may be workable with males, the consensus is that it is not essential for everyone on a female team to love each other. Insisting upon it may be unnecessary at best and counterproductive at worst.

Female athletes must feel loved. Loving our players and making sure they are aware of our commitment to do so no matter what is something that cannot be mailed in. The female softball player must understand that you love her. Communicating this same level of love to a male athlete may be unnecessary. Fairness, opportunity, respect: these are what males look for. Love from their coach, on the other hand, may not be a priority for them.

Respect for her coach is a fragile commodity for the female athlete. It is critical that her coach be worthy of respect. Behavior that is cruel, biased, or disappointing will dash her respect on the rocks. The threshold for the coach managing male athletes is higher. A male athlete can compartmentalize different aspects of his coach's life and overlook behavior that may diminish respect. As long as the opportunity to play exists, the male athletes may overlook bad behavior. Not so with our female athletes. They hold us to a high standard of behavior, and if it is respect we seek from them, we must be cognizant of this reality.

Though there are many differences in the way we must approach coaching men and women, there are constants that apply to both. Athletes of both genders demand a coach who possesses competency, who knows their sport and how to teach it. Athletes are drawn to coaches who are leaders, regardless of their particular style. And finally, all athletes seek a coach who can motivate them, one who is able to reach in and bring out their very best performance.

Chapter 10

Profiles in Great Coaching

The principles of coaching softball players advocated in this book may seem undoable, not possible under the real-world parameters of having to run a winning program. While none among us can execute all of them perfectly, we have before us many who come close.

Coach Wade Wilson—Texas Lutheran University

One such coach is Texas Lutheran University (TLU) Head Coach Wade Wilson. As the winner of the 2019 NCAA Division III National Championship, it is obvious that Wade knows the game. He and his staff were the recipients of the 2019 NFCA DIII Coaching Staff of the Year. What is not so obvious is the foundation of connection, love, and leadership he has laid at TLU. Now in his ninth season with the Bulldogs, Wade came straight from the high school ranks, setting about to put TLU on the college softball map.

Listen to the words his players use to describe the love he has for them:

"He wanted to be involved in our lives, on and off the field because he really did care about each and every one of us."

"Coach Wilson genuinely cared about our well-being as people, not just players on a softball team."

"He was available to us not just as our coach, but also as a mentor."

Even though these are glowing testimonials, there is a toughness, a competitive side of Coach Wilson, and this aspect of his coaching style was met with similar praise:

"Coach Wilson is fiery, competitive and determined to win. When you are on the softball field it is always business. He is what most would describe as a tough coach...."

Chapter 10. Profiles in Great Coaching

"There are very few times Coach Wilson just hands out high fives or 'atta babies' and I respect him for that because I'm a firm believer in 'not everything deserves a trophy.'"

"He pushed us, because he loved us."

"He's tough because he truly cares."

So we see a picture of a caring, loving coach who is brimming with competitiveness, demanding everything from his players. Coach Wilson realizes the value of coupling love for his players with the requirement that they put forth maximum effort.

His players give him the highest tribute:

"Outside of the softball field Coach Wilson was like a second father figure to his players."

"I will forever be thankful for the love that Coach Wilson showed me when I was a player and the love he continues to show me now. He has made a lasting impact on my life and I will always respect and love him as well."

Coach Wilson uses but never overuses praise. His words of appreciation flow freely to those who earn them through their effort and attitude. One of his players explains: "Coach Wilson wasn't one to sing your praises all the time, and we didn't need him to. When he took the time to tell you that you had a good game or when he would send a text saying he was proud of you, you knew that you had earned it." He expressed his appreciation for his players, giving them credit for his success as a coach: "Our coach was always sure to remind us how grateful he was for us, because without us he wouldn't be able to do what he is so passionate about doing—coaching, teaching, and loving his athletes."

A former TLU pitcher tells of how took her from a player who had lost her fire for the game to earning All-American honors:

I had the pleasure of playing for Coach Wilson the last two years of my softball career. He added me to his roster as a prior Division I transfer who had fallen out of love with the game. In playing for Coach Wilson, I quickly regained my burning passion to compete. A feeling I thought I couldn't get back. He humbled me, challenged me, made me a smarter pitcher and taught me the value in being a selfless teammate. Although Coach Wilson enjoys winning, this was not his top priority. Above all, he expected us to be high quality individuals. Beyond his undeniable success on the field, Coach Wilson made me a better person. Whether it be tough games I couldn't seem to work my way out

> of, or unpleasant life seasons, he was present and showing me how to navigate the situation in the most respectable way.
>   After my junior year softball season, I was honored with an All-American award. This award calls for a small ceremony in Oklahoma City in which all Division III All-Americans are acknowledged. However, my family could not make the ceremony. I had no way of getting there and no one to stand next to me while receiving such an important award in my career as a pitcher. Our coaching staff drove me from Seguin, Texas, to Oklahoma City and ensured that I would be celebrated for my efforts on the field. It was a day I will never forget. I felt extremely cared for and appreciated as a student-athlete.
>   I am lucky to know Coach Wilson. I will continue to honor him daily by being the hardest working employee, best sister, loving daughter and consistent friend that I can be.

From her words we see a coach who is intentional. His goal is to elevate his players as people. Her final paragraph underscores the impact he had on her life. He changed her, helper to grow as a person. Her life is better because of her coach.

Another TLU alumni writes of a relationship that has endured long after her playing days were over. Coach Wilson continues to care for and mentor her:

> I think what sets Wilson apart is his ability to build independent relationships with each of his players that transcend the game. Before playing two years at TLU I transferred from a junior college. I loved my JUCO coach but I have not heard from him since the day I left. I am currently an ER nurse and have received three messages of encouragement and well wishes just in the past month from Wilson. Two years after I stepped off the field for the last time, it is evident that my coach valued me not only as a player but as a person. Thats how you reach female athletes and that's how you succeed as their coach!

A TLU catcher points out how Coach Wilson used different approaches with different players. He understood the differences in personality types and what approach would reach each individual player:

> I honestly don't know where to start. Maybe a quick background of myself so you can see why Coach Wilson made (and continues to make) a huge impact on my life. I started at TLU as a freshman in 2012 and played through my senior year (2016). I am a pretty shy, quiet person and it takes awhile for me to open up and make friends. So my freshman year was a challenge, to say the least, as I started a new phase of my life, at a new school, that was 3 hours away from home,

Chapter 10. Profiles in Great Coaching

where I knew absolutely no one. Softball gave me the opportunity to actually be around people but it still took some time for me to warm up. Coach Wilson could probably tell you but I might have said maybe 5 words to him the entire year. However, by my Junior and Senior year, you couldn't shut me up.

I am now an accountant by day, so I am by no means an expert on what it takes to be a great coach but I've been around enough coaches in my 16-year softball career to know when one is special. Coach Wilson was one, without a doubt. Coach Wilson was a tough coach. He has an eye for talent and he doesn't let you be anything less then the player he knows you are. He also somehow knows the best way to do that. Girls tend to handle criticism differently. Some respond better to being screamed at and some need the silent treatment and some need direction on how to do better next time. I for one do not respond well to being yelled at. Quiet people, like myself, do more internalizing than others. I would beat myself up more than anyone else would. Coach Wilson somehow knew that. Out of my four years there, I never got one of his "ass chewings," and that's not because I didn't do anything to earn one (I'm far from perfect). And the people who did get one were the people who responded well to it.

This ability to home in on the unique mental and emotional characteristics of each player is a quality shared by all great coaches. This catcher continues in her praise for Coach Wilson, explaining his two sides: the tough no nonsense coach and the warm, caring father figure:

> Coach Wilson has two sides to him. From the outside looking in, he's a tough coach that strives for perfection and is determined to win. And when we are out at the field, I would say that's true. But when we leave the field for the day, he becomes someone different. He becomes the person we can go to to talk about anything. He's the person that can help us through when we are going through something rough. He's there, he's present, no matter what. Coach Wilson become a father figure to me while I was away from home, and I still to this day see that to be true. He continues to follow up with me and my life. When I go back to TLU to watch games he's always happy and excited for me to be there. He continues to make me feel like I'm still a part of his team, even though I haven't been for the past 4 years. I trust this man with my life.

A member of the 2019 TLU National Championship team reflects on the lessons Coach Wilson taught his players and the tangible ways he showed how he cared for them:

Coaching Women's Softball

> There is so much that can be said about Coach Wilson but I'll try to keep it short. Coach Wilson is the type of coach that is tough and expects a lot out of us all the time but one who also cares about us as players like his own family. Coach Wilson is one of the most "tell it like it is" coaches that I've ever had and though it was hard to handle sometimes, I appreciate his honesty. He taught us so much more than the game of softball and for that I am grateful. As a player, I can appreciate a coach that doesn't care just about wins and losses but cares about other lessons that can be learned like how to handle tough criticism, and how to be mentally tough in the midst of failure. At practice day in and day out, one thing that he always preached to us was being a selfless teammate. He always made it a point to pose the question, "What will people remember about you, not in terms of batting average or fielding percentage but as a person and as a teammate. How did you make the people around you feel? What will people remember about you as a player when you leave this place?" I think those questions helped shaped my career as a TLU softball player because I was put in the position where I had to decide what kind of teammate I wanted to be remembered as and I think it has affected me still to this day.

The lessons he emphasized shaped this player beyond the field. His influence for good continues up to the present time. She goes on to tell of how Coach Wilson took tangible action that backed up his words. He preached that the past TLU players had a part in the accomplishment of winning the 2019 National Championship. He included those players in the success of the team, reinforcing his relationship with his former players.

> TLU softball is very big on family atmosphere and with Coach Wilson that was no different. We always talked about how we were playing for the past, the present and the future bulldogs. That saying became our motto, especially in the 2019 season. After we won the National Championship, I really saw that motto come to life, especially with Coach Wilson. I think in my time at TLU, the most respectable and honorable thing that Coach Wilson did was giving a National Championship trophy to every single past player that had come through the program and played under him because he decided that we were able to succeed in that moment in that year because of everything that those previous players had accomplished, which is true. Life goes on and softball eventually ends, but one thing I know to be true is that I am thankful for having a coach

Chapter 10. Profiles in Great Coaching

like Coach Wilson. I couldn't imagine my time at TLU with anyone else.

Texas Lutheran players obviously have the highest level of respect for their coach. We need to know how Coach Wilson sets about earning and keeping his players' respect. He sums up his game plan:

> I treat our players like I treat any other human. Relationships take time to grow and for a trust to be formed. I always try to be honest and want them to be the same. Sometimes us coaches have to say things that hurt the feelings of our players. We say often that when we are on the field or in a team setting that you cannot take our coaching personal. We have to push buttons and sometimes criticism is needed for growth. This is much easier for an athlete to take when they trust you as a person first.

When asked what he does to establish himself as the leader of the team, his plan is to involve the entire team and coaching staff in representing and promoting the program they are all a part of: "As the head coach I'd love it if all of our players were leaders. I'm always conscious about referring to 'our' program and 'our' players, 'our' team. It's not my team; it's the players' team and we are all representing Texas Lutheran University. I don't ask our players or our assistants to do anything that I wouldn't do. When the players and assistants are given ownership, they tend to take more pride in what we are doing."

Coach Wilson encourages competition as the means to extract maximum effort from his players: "We try and put as much competition around them as possible. Ideally they are having to compete every day to keep their position or pushing the player in front of them. I've never been a big rah rah coach. If they are not working hard enough they don't see the field."

His own competitive nature pushes him to improve his skills as a softball coach: "I watch and try and learn from others that are having success. We all steal ideas and drills from one another. I'm not afraid to try new things even if we feel uncomfortable doing them. If it works, great; if not, move onto the next. Most coaches do the same things every day, just some do it better than others."

Coach Wilson is a coach to be emulated. He knows the game, connects with his players, loves them, and leads them. He is sure to give them his praise and appreciation when warranted, and he has their unquestioned respect. His impressive record as a coach traces back to all of these things.

Coaching Women's Softball

Danielle Zymkowitz—The University of Wisconsin

In her fourth season with the University of Wisconsin, Associate Head Coach Danielle Zymkowitz is recognized as a great coaching talent. Her coaching has elevated the offensive level of the Badgers program, helping them to consecutive NCAA tournament appearances in 2017, 2018, and 2019. As Badgers head coach Yvette Healy puts it, "Danielle's character, energy, enthusiasm, ability to motivate others and creative approach to teaching the game makes her a rising star in the coaching profession" (University of Wisconsin Softball webpage: uwbadgers.com).

Danielle has an enviable resume as a player from her days as a two-time All-American at the University of Illinois to All-NPF honors as a member of the Chicago Bandits. Yet it is not her great breath of knowledge of the game or her skills as a teacher alone that make her stand out. Her love for the game and for the players under her charge is her trademark.

As an outfielder in the Badger program writes: "I always felt like she was in my corner and wanted the best for me."

Coach Z is able to instill that level of confidence so critical to success on and off the field. Another player speaks of how Coach Z changed her attitude towards adversity: "She changed my outlook during tough times and made me realize the little victories in situations."

She inspired hard work in her players by working hard herself, according to this All-Region infielder: "Her contagious energy and the hard work she put in to push me is the main way she connected with me."

An outfielder sums up what makes Coach Z so popular with her players: "The biggest factor that makes her an awesome coach is her love for the game and her love for our team."

A Badger infielder writes of Coach Z's leadership and her ability to understand her players individually:

> Having Coach Z as a coach and mentor for the past four years has been one of the greatest blessings. It was amazing having a coach who exhibited the same passion and drive as I had as a player. We know she has our back as players and as people no matter what, teaching us to be true, to trust ourselves, and to play and act with a committed heart. Her obvious love for the game along with her energetic and down to

Chapter 10. Profiles in Great Coaching

earth personality was very easy to get on board with as soon as we met her. Throughout my four years playing for Coach Z, we've had ups and downs, frustrations, injuries, epiphanies, and incredible successes. She understands that every player is different—every swing, throw, biomechanics, and personality are different—and we know how hard she works to understand each of us. Coach Z and I are very similar in our leadership styles, work ethic, and that we love everything about softball and baseball, and she has contributed immensely to my maturity as a player, leader, and person.

She continues to tell of how Coach Z provided wisdom and reassurance when it was needed:

There are several conversations with Coach Z that I will never forget, but one of the most memorable was the first heart-to-heart conversation we had in the fall of my redshirt freshman year. I was still rehabbing from a major injury from the year prior, and I could not play at all yet. During practice, we all went around explaining our "why" for playing softball. I said I play because I love it with everything I have, and all I wanted was to be able to go all out and give my all for the game that had given me so much. I could barely get out my answer through tears from the frustration of my injury. In my next individual [meeting], Coach Z expressed her appreciation for how I showed my passion for the game and how that love for the game is going to bring great things in my career. It was one of the first moments she got to know the type of player I am and how much I love the game before she had seen me play any softball, and how similar we are in our passion for softball. It was one of the first times in my young collegiate career where I really felt understood and she was right—loving the game and putting in the work gave us some incredible, unforgettable moments as a team.

Another Badger, an All-American Scholar Athlete tells of a time when Coach Z had just the right, insightful words of encouragement:

I was a pitcher in college, but if I am being completely honest most of my time was spent in the bullpen rather on the field. My role was to connect with hitters, be a leader off the field for my teammates and work with my coaches to enhance our student athlete experience. Some would say it was a waste of my talent to go to a big D I school when I could've been successful at a smaller school; one of my coaches along the way did say those words believe it or not. And I felt that after my freshman year of college, the pressure was real after getting a total of 6 innings, but I loved my school and my teammates and I wanted to work my butt off to get pitching time.

My first practice of my sophomore year we were introduced to our new coach—Danielle Z. She was quiet. Barely said more than two sentences within her first couple of weeks. After a bad practice a month in I had stayed a little late to help pick up our indoor facility and Coach Z was hanging out. She looked at me and said, "I don't know your story, but I do know that someone along the way told you that you couldn't do this but I promise you, you can." Not only was I completely shocked by the fact that she was the one who talked to me, but by the words she said. Before I could respond she said, "I used to go into our facility and do extra work almost every day. Your teammates notice you, I notice you. You stayed here to help pick up, you help the hitters by feeding the machine, you care about this program—Don't you ever think that the small things go unnoticed because it's the glue that helps to hold this all together."

I knew this person 3 weeks—a hitting coach, someone who I was not directly working with, knew all the right things to say in a matter of minutes. She was so diligent in her first couple of weeks at Wisconsin that she was not just watching everyone to see their softball abilities but who are they as teammates. And more importantly, as people.

Coach Z takes a thoughtful approach to earning and keeping her players' respect. She lets them know from the beginning of their relationship that she as a coach respects them as a player:

> I think that you can learn just as much or even more from your players than what you can teach them. When the student-athlete first gets on campus, I like to ask them a ton of questions to get a better understanding of their game. I would say that I earn their respect by first respecting their game and all the work that they have done to get to where they currently are. I would also say that I am a player's coach. I love to be in the cages with them and especially in the fight with them when they are competing in the box. I am mentally with them every pitch, trying. If we are working on a hitting approach together and it doesn't work, I am the first one to take responsibility for it. That is how I believe I can keep their respect. This game is a game of failure, and there are many times that I also fail as a coach. I put my ego aside, showing that it will never be about me, and just get back to work focusing on the most important piece: the player.

Coach Z does two things that characterize great leaders. She serves those she leads, and she leads by doing rather than by talking about leadership: "My version of leadership is probably a little different than most.

Chapter 10. Profiles in Great Coaching

I love to serve. I love to show up every day and invest in the players. I lead by example by getting to practice early to set up, pick up balls with them in the cage, shag in the outfield, and be there after practice if they want more reps. Whatever I could do to help, count me in. I don't really say much about leadership, instead I just show them how much I love them by serving them."

Coach Z motivates her players by challenging them with innovative practice routines and by sharing her own vision with them:

> I love to challenge them in everything they do. I love to put the hack attacks on 70 mph in the cages so that their practices are harder than the games. I believe I do this as a coach because as a player I loved to crank up the machine to prepare for Monica Abbott and the other hard throwers in the NPF. It gave me the confidence to stand tall in the box against someone who overmatched me. As a coach, I instill confidence in them by sharing my vision with them. I let them know that I believe they can hit the pitch and show them the process needed to get there. Once they believe and get the hang of the drill, when they face a pitcher throwing 65 they feel more prepared.

Coach Z puts in the work, upgrading her knowledge and competency as a coach:

> I love to learn even more now than I did when I was in school. I love to read about people and great leaders. Success leaves clues. As coaches, we are not rewriting the wheel; there are many greats that came before us. Attending and listening to coaches speak at the ABCA or NFCA is always a highlight of my year. I feel honored when I get to learn from them because they are so passionate about their field. Lastly, I love to watch baseball and softball on TV not just for the enjoyment of the game, but I am watching the little things inside the game (the shifts, the pitch sequences, base running, footwork).

One University of Wisconsin player and Big Ten Player of the Year speaks of her strong connection with Coach Z: "The coach that I feel I connected most with and that has most significantly influenced my 'everyday' is one of my most current coaches. We call her Z or Coach Z. She played softball in college at the University of Illinois, and then continued to play in the pro league for several years after that. Z still holds the highest batting average in a season of over .600. What's crazy is she is a remarkable player, yes, but I would vouch for her being an even better leader and person." She continues in her praise, explaining how Coach Z's impact on her players is directly related to her own work ethic:

> The way she approaches her work is second to none. I've never seen anything like it. It inspires me. At first, I thought she had an unhealthy obsession for the game. But I've come to realize she knows what she loves to play, coach, and watch, and she was able to find a way to make it her career. I hope someday I am able to do the same thing. Z also has more passion for the game than anyone I've met; now that she's not playing, all she cares about is helping make the game better. She focuses on the small things and helps people's love and respect for the game grow every day. Not only is her love for the game contagious, but her positive attitude and kid-like energy are as well.

The player pays Coach Z the ultimate compliment—she strives to emulate her in several different areas of life:

> Z made me change the way I look at the role of a coach. She helped me realize that a coach is someone we respect, admire and strive to be like. Some traits she has that I admire or strive to emulate are her interpersonal communication skills, her passion for what she does, her servant leadership skills, her never settle mentality, her quest for knowledge, and her desire to always give back—to both the community and next generation. Because of Z, I approach each day with a grateful heart. I wake up wanting to tackle the day and realize today is another day to impact people's lives. I see each interaction I have with someone as a chance to be vulnerable, genuine, and unapologetically myself. I see opportunities throughout my day that I once may have taken for granted, and now I invest in the small things more rigorously.

She sums up the reason for Coach Z's success as a coach: "What I feel like ultimately connected us the most is Z's concern / heart for people. Softball is important but taking care of and empowering us as young women is something she makes a priority."

Charlie Dobbins—William Peace University

William Peace University Head Coach brings a rich softball pedigree to the job. Prior to his twenty years at WPU, he was the catcher for the world famous "King and His Court," traveling the world for a decade. With over 400 wins to his credit at WPU, his program is a perennial Division III contender. A two-sport college athlete himself, Coach Dobbins brings a strong competitive spirit to his team.

Chapter 10. Profiles in Great Coaching

Those who know Charlie or have even met him realize what a great ambassador he is for our sport. His players consider it a privilege to be coached by this knowledgeable yet warm and personable coach. His players testify that he takes his responsibility as a mentor and an example very seriously: "He was very passionate about being a good role model so that I would strive to be a better version of myself."

He promoted a true family atmosphere at WPU to create memories cherished by this alumna: "The sense of family that was given when I played at Peace was like no other."

One of his former players explains how Coach Dobbins is known for his compassion and for caring about his players. In spite of having a knowledge of the game unmatched by most coaches, it is the person Charlie Dobbins that his players value most:

> As hard headed as he may be, he has one of the biggest hearts of anyone I know.
>
> He knows every little thing about everyone and checks in on you just to stay updated on the littlest things sometimes, but is always there when the big stuff comes around too.
>
> Regardless of what it was, everything that ever happened my coach was right there to either tell me he was proud of me, or tell me we'd get through it.

Another former player sums up the consensus of his players' feelings about him: "I can't say enough good things about him, to be honest."

Coach Dobbins views gaining the respect of his players as a process, one in which different players build trust at different rates:

> The key is that trust must be developed between the coaches and the team, and on an individual level between coach and player. Every player on the team does not miraculously start trusting you at the same time; you must establish trust with each player on your team and that can occur at different times throughout the season. This happens in two ways, one as a coach, and the other as a person. Coach "K" probably said it best: "Coaching is about relationships. It goes way beyond X's and O's. You must create an environment of trust among your staff and athletes. Without trust, you have nothing. If you do have trust, you will be able to accomplish great things." Always be caring and consistent. Not every kid is going to buy in to everything you teach. They are not all going to have the same skill set. This also applies to your assistant coaches and staff. They must trust you, and you must trust them. If you work hard in building confidence, your teams will stay committed to your goals.

Coaching Women's Softball

Coach Dobbins's leadership style is based on welcoming input, sharing credit for success, and taking responsibility for mistakes that might have been made:

> The best leaders do not make it about themselves. I give those under me the chance to show off their skills. Other people's success (your assistant coaches, players) does not diminish mine. I try to be generous with praise and give credit where it is due. I respect the opinions of my assistant coaches and team and am always ready to listen when someone suggests a different approach to doing things.
>
> When things go wrong, and they will, step up and own it. My name is on the lineup card. Taking responsibility does not just mean admitting that you made a mistake; rather, it involves being accountable for the consequences of what happened and then doing your best to make things right. You cannot change what happened; it is what you do afterward that makes all the difference.

Coach Dobbins places great importance on listening and gaining input from his players: "Always communicate well, but also focus on your ability to listen. This allows you to evaluate from a different perspective and understand a different view. This gives you time to reflect and make an appropriate response."

He quantifies the behaviors necessary to be a true leader, naming them "Tools to establish yourself as leader of your team":

> Always be loyal
> Maintain a professional image
> Keep a positive attitude with laser focus
> Be a student, continue to learn
> Always be honest
> Encourage everyone through your confidence

Coach Dobbins utilizes individual attention, both with him and his assistants, as a means to motivate his players to excel: "We focus on a lot of one on one time. This takes pressure off the 'team' experience, and we can focus on each person's strength and weakness. These one on one times allow us to get a better snapshot of the individual, and it strengthens the relationship between player and coach."

He cites the wise use of resources as key to developing players: "Provide the resources to do the job. Do not miss out by not providing the needed tools to make the players better. Be creative, this can be accomplished in all kinds of ways, and stay in budget. Actively involve

Chapter 10. Profiles in Great Coaching

players and your assistant coaches. I believe one of the reasons we have been successful, is that I assign my assistant coaches' responsibility to specific positions based to history and skill set. Now the player has an opportunity to work one on one with their position coach, who is going to have major input towards playing times, etc."

Coach Dobbins takes a progressive attitude towards learning new ways to teach. Likening coaching to teaching brings his focus on to the player as a student and the coach as a professor:

> I believe coaching is a form of teaching and we are all educators just like a professor at our University. Get involved in the NFCA, serve on committees. Learn about the NCAA, serve on committees. We all do camps and recruit but stay up to speed with the technology that changes every year.
>
> Listen to your assistant coaches, be open to "new ways" to teach the same old thing. Be willing to listen, and open to change. Remember the old saying, the definition of insanity is doing something the same way over and over and expecting a different result.

A former player speaks of the things that make Charlie a great coach in her eyes. His intense love of the game is inspirational, his knowledge of it nearly exhaustive, and his humility so apparent that he is truly a great coach:

> To me, one thing that sets him apart from other coaches is his true love of the game. He really, really, loves softball—coaching it, playing it, watching it, talking about it. When you are around him and talking anything softball, you can see the excitement and passion in his eyes. His love of the game has impacted and influenced so many other people—it's the reason I still play several times a week, and got married on the softball field at Peace! By sharing his passion for the game, it helps him build trust with his teams. It's one thing to show up and coach because it's your job and you have to be there; it's another to get to go out and do your favorite thing every day.
>
> Another thing that makes him so good at his job is his knowledge of the sport. A constant learner by nature and walking rule book. He's played almost every position on the field which allows him to understand and teach the mental side of playing. We used to get into arguments on the field when I was playing second base. He'd tell me to shade to the right or left, and I would say, no, I like being here! After running many laps and debating if I should switch to being a track star, I finally started paying attention and thinking about why he was asking me to move over. It wasn't because he didn't like where I was standing; it was because the pitch that

he was calling for had a high probability of being hit in the hole, and he wanted me to be in the right position to field it. He teaches more than just the physical skills needed to play the game at a high level.

I think the last thing to say about Coach Dobbins would be that even with all the success he's had, he stays humble. He doesn't take the glory or spotlight when his team wins, he gives it all to his players. He makes you want to keep coming back and learn more about the game, grow your skills, and hopefully, win. He is there for his players, willing to stay after practice or games to work on hitting or hit some ground balls. and he is there for them off the field too, making sure his players truly embody the term "student athlete." He knows not everyone is going to have a career playing or coaching softball, so it is important have a plan (or backup plan) to be successful in life—which is the great game of them all.

Jana McGinnis—Jacksonville State University

Jacksonville State University Head Coach Jana McGinnis serves as an example of a coach who mentors her players while achieving great success on the field. In her twenty-seven-year tenure at the helm of the Gamecocks program, this six-time Ohio Valley Conference Coach of the Year has amassed over 900 wins.

For those of us who know her, even more impressive than her knowledge of the sport or her extreme competitiveness is her character. She is an intentional mentor and is known by her players as a coach who cares deeply about each one of them. Her former players span the professions, including many who coach in high schools across the South. JSU softball alumni speak of Coach with an almost reverent tone, now recognizing the effort she put forth to connect with, love, and lead these young women.

A former Gamecocks infielder and Ohio Valley Conference (OVC) Player of the Year explains how Coach McGinnis tailored her approach to motivating each player on the team:

> Coach has a way of learning her players quickly; learning which ones to push and which ones to encourage. I was a player that performed better with a little push. Coach took time to get to know me as a person, and let me know that she cared about me. She also took the time to let me know what her expectations were for me. She pushed me to be the best me that I could be, and did not accept less even when I would have. She did not baby me or believe I deserved special

Chapter 10. Profiles in Great Coaching

treatment because I was a female athlete. She just wanted us to be treated as equal to the men's teams.

The record seven-time OVC Player of the Week speaks of the great respect the team had for Coach McGinnis and how she earned that respect by genuinely caring for her players:

> Within a few minutes of being around the team as a freshman, you quickly become aware of the level of respect given to Coach. And it doesn't take long being around her to understand why she is so respected. The fear of disappointing Coach had an impact on your actions both on and off the field. However, she didn't earn your respect through fear and scare tactics. She earned each player's respect by proving she cared for each individual person, and who you were going to be after ball was over. Ball was just the vehicle to preparing you for the rest of your life.

An All-Conference Gamecocks pitcher gives us a window into what it was like to play for Coach McGinnis:

> Playing for Coach McGinnis was the smartest decision I have ever made for many reasons, but this one stands out from the others ... she cared about where we ended up as adults and saw it as her job to prepare us for success in every walk of life. Of course, OVC Championships were a nice bonus, but having a coach that knew you and your heart was even greater. She knew exactly who to push and how far; as well as who to hug and tell them that they were loved. She made connections with her players that were an unbreakable bond. I don't know if it was a practiced art that she had perfected but she did so naturally. I later found out that Coach lived by her faith and that's why she was able to do this with us so easily. She was spreading God's love in all of our lives.
>
> The word I would use to describe Coach McGinnis would be "SAINT."

She goes on to explain how Coach McGinnis motivated her players: "She was one of those people you hate to let down, not out of fear or punishment, but because she was so good at heart. You trusted her and knew that it was safe to do so. You worked for her because you knew she was working tirelessly too. You show up every single day, despite the sore muscles, because she showed up every day too."

She speaks of the incredibly high level of respect JSU players had for Coach McGinnis: "I have never been a part of a team where 100 percent of the players respect the head coach to the highest point possible.

Coaching Women's Softball

In my years playing at JSU, not once did I hear a teammate speak poorly about her; it was always praise and positives. It seems euphoric with this description, but it represents her heart and approach to the fullest."

Finally, she provides words that give us the essence of Coach McGinnis:

> She is a rare coach, definitely not a sales woman. She is pure, honest, and sets high expectations (but not out of reach). She molds you not only into an OVC Champion, but a successful woman in the adult world. She cares about where her players end up and wants to see them become life-long champions in world without the sport of softball. That, to me, is what sets her apart from every other coach. She invests into every single person that walks through her door and gives them 100 percent each day, just as she does for her family. Being a Gamecock means so much more than the sport of softball; it's a way of life. Thank you, Coach McGinnis, for setting your program apart from all the others. YOU make it a special place!

Coach McGinnis cites respect as a cornerstone of her program: "This means that it is absolutely needed in order to have a successful program There are a few things that are essential for a program to be successful, but without respect there can be no success."

Coach McGinnis goes about earning that respect by setting high standards for her players, and meeting those standards in her own life: "I feel like I am a coach that sets high standards for each of our players. In order to give them the drive to reach those standards, I must do the same for myself. I try to live as an example. I try to do as I say. I do not ask anything out of our players that I do not ask out of myself. I hope they see me as an honest, fair and consistent human being. And most important, a person that puts God first in my life!"

It is interesting that she describes leadership as a commitment to the program's greater good while ensuring that she values and care for each individual player:

> I really think a leader makes those around them better. I hope I do more leading by my actions than what I say. I always put the team/program first. That means making very difficult decisions at times, not the easiest ones. I try to engage and communicate with each player in their own special way. They are each unique and different, but at the end of the day, they all know that I care about each one of them the same. I see each special talent as a gift to our team and program. They understand that Team is ALL of us.

Chapter 10. Profiles in Great Coaching

Perhaps one measure of the effectiveness of a coach is whether they are able to motivate their team, to bring out the best possible in each player. Coach McGinnis uses the platform of her players' respect for her to challenge them. Informing them that her purpose is to bring out the best in them as an athlete and as an individual, she gains access to push, praise, and to correct when needed:

> I hope they become self driven or motivated by the respect we have built for each other. When the players earn my respect, it motivates me to work hard every day to make them the best. I tell them from the start that my job is to get the best out of them as a player and person. That may mean pushing, pulling, carrying, or just walking beside them. I am honest with them. When the players do good, I tell them. But when they are not bringing their best, I will tell them as well. It is not always praise. Players at the end of the day appreciate a Coach that will hold them accountable and be honest with them.

Perhaps Coach McGinnis's greatest asset is her humble teachability. Although she is among the most successful coaches in college softball, she listens and learns from a variety of sources, including her players. Evolving in this way has enabled her to remain at the top of the game for over a quarter of a century:

> I read a lot when it comes to learning more about skill improvement. Whether it is books or articles. I also watch videos. Early in my career, I went to coaching clinics. But as my family grew and I tried to have more home time, I found other ways to get new information. My favorite and best way is to just talk and share ideas with my coaching friends. I have so many friends that are much more successful than myself. I love learning from them. I am a true believer that we can learn from any successful person, no matter what sport they coach or what occupation they are in. There are always qualities that each has that I can work to have. I also watch documentaries on successful people. I also learn from my assistant coaches. I appreciate any thing they can add to making our program or team better. And, this may sound strange, but I learn from our players. A player may come into our program and may have been taught a skill totally different than what we teach. I first ask for feedback from the player. Like, why do you do it this way? Why is it a better way? I will never know everything about our sport. It is constantly evolving and growing.

Index

Arizona State University 59

Baylor University 30, 37
Berg, Laura 32–33, 45, 89, 152–153
Big 10 Conference 23
Birmingham Southern College 57, 76, 115, 140
Bucknell University 102

Cassidy, Kimball 57, 76, 115, 140
Chrietzberg, Casey 64–66
Christopher Newport University 46, 146
College Coaches 7, 136, 138
competing 36–38, 41–44
Constantinesco, Kim 4
criticism 19, 102

Davenport, Mike 78–79, 129
Dillingham, JJ. 22, 56
Dobbins, Charlie 72–74, 92, 125–126, 139, 148, 152–154, 166–170
Dorrence, Anson 4, 8, 20–21, 79–80, 103, 157

East Texas Baptist University 32, 60
Elliot, Brandon 28–29

Federal Bureau of Alcohol, Tobacco, Firearms and Explosives 3, 63, 77, 93, 149
Foster, Courtnay 84, 85, 102

Generation Z 14–15, 92
Grindrod, Tracy 12–13, 46, 82, 183
Guthrie, Joe 15–16, 41, 137–138, 148

Harkins, Taylor 1–2

Jacksonville State University 117, 129, 132–133, 170

Kolaitis, Jimmy 10–11, 66, 145, 147, 151

Lilley, Jenna 66–68, 147
Lipscomb University 22

Matos, Francisco 139
McGinnis, Jana 117, 129, 132–133, 170–173
Moore, Glenn 30

National Professional Fastpitch (NPF) 48–49

Oregon State University 32, 45

PAC 12 Conference 21, 25, 56
Parr, Keith 46, 146
Pennsylvania State University 15–16

recruiting 18–19

Shirley, Janae 32–34
Smith, Beverly 87–89
Snead State Community College 12–13, 46, 82
Snyder, Craig 14–15
social media 19
Studeman, Les 57

Team USA 21, 66
Tee, Jason 3
Texas Lutheran University 115, 145, 156
Texas Rangers 139
Thatcher, Karen 120–121
Toledo, Cheri 4
Trevecca Nazarene University 45, 87
Tyree, Ben 45, 87

United States Olympic Team 32, 45
University of Alabama at Birmingham 15, 41, 85, 102, 138, 148
University of North Georgia 78, 129
University of South Carolina 87–89
University of Tennessee 116
University of Texas at Tyler 30
University of Wisconsin 48, 143, 152, 162

Virginia Wesleyan University 28

Wafer, Cristin (Vitek) 37–38
William Peace University 72, 81, 92, 125, 152, 166
Wilson, Wade 115–116, 145, 156–161

Zymkowitz, Danielle 48–49, 143–144, 162–166

www.ingramcontent.com/pod-product-compliance
Ingram Content Group UK Ltd.
Pitfield, Milton Keynes, MK11 3LW, UK
UKHW042015140426
5217IPUK00015B/1194